Lords of
Battle

OSPREY
PUBLISHING

Lords of Battle

The World of the Celtic Warrior

STEPHEN ALLEN

First published in Great Britain in 2007 by Osprey Publishing,
Midland House, West Way, Botley, Oxford OX2 0PH, United Kingdom.
443 Park Avenue South, New York, NY 10016, USA.
Email: info@ospreypublishing.com

Every attempt has been made by the Publishers to secure the appropriate permissions for materials reproduced in
this book. If there has been any oversight we will be happy to rectify the situation and written submission should
be made to the Publishers.

A CIP catalogue record for this book is available from the British Library

ISBN: 978 1 84176 948 6

Page layout by Ken Vail Graphic Design, Cambridge, UK
Typeset in Truesdell and Celtic
Maps by The Map Studio
Originated by United Graphics Ltd, Singapore
Printed in China through Worldprint Ltd
Index by Alan Thatcher

07 08 09 10 11   10 9 8 7 6 5 4 3 2 1

For a catalogue of all books published by Osprey please contact:

NORTH AMERICA
Osprey Direct c/o Random House Distribution Center, 400 Hahn Road,
Westminster, MD 21157, USA
E-mail: info@ospreydirect.com

ALL OTHER REGIONS
Osprey Direct UK, P.O. Box 140, Wellingborough, Northants, NN8 2FA, UK
E-mail: info@ospreydirect.co.uk

www.ospreypublishing.com

Front cover: Detail from Battersea shield. (Werner Forman Archive / British Museum)
Title page: A gold torc from the Snettisham horde. (Werner Forman Archive / British Museum)
Back cover: Celtic knot design. (© Courtney Davis, www.celtic-art.com)
Endpapers: Fort Dun Aengus. (Werner Forman Archive)

Acknowledgements: My sincere thanks to all who have helped in the preparation of this book, especially to Anita
and Julie at Osprey Publishing, whose support and encouragement have been invaluable; and to my wife, whose
patience over the past year has been boundless. Lords of Battle is dedicated to her.

Dedication: To Françoise.

CONTENTS

WHO WERE THE CELTS?

The whole race ... is war-mad, and both high-spirited and quick for battle ... and if roused they come together all at once for the struggle, ready to risk their lives with nothing to help them but might and daring. (Strabo, Geography)

This is how the Greek historian and geographer Strabo described the Celtic peoples of western Europe in the 1st century BC. In so doing, he reflected the popular attitude of the Mediterranean world towards its wild, uncivilized neighbours. To the classical civilizations of Greece and Rome, the Celtic warrior represented the archetypal barbarian: huge in stature, immensely strong and bloodthirsty beyond belief. Charging naked into battle, impervious to wounds, and wielding a terrible sword with which to take the heads of his enemies, he was the antithesis of the drilled and disciplined soldiers of the Greek hoplite phalanx or the Roman legion. This powerful image is still with us after more than two millennia. It is so strong that it is often difficult to see beyond it and to discover the real nature of the Celtic warrior as an essential element in the structure and maintenance of ancient Celtic society. The society in which he lived, fought and died was vibrant, rich and complex. It endured for over 500 years across much of Europe and has left us a legacy that we can experience in art, language and legend.

How to define the Celts continues to be a subject of controversy and often heated debate among academics and laymen alike, and for many people can be a very emotive issue. The term 'Celts' – *Keltoi* in Greek and *Celtae* in Latin – was first used by the Greek geographer Hecataeus of Miletus to describe the barbarian tribes living near the Greek colony of Massalia, the modern French city of Marseille on the Mediterranean coast of France, almost 2,600 years ago. He also wrote that Narbo (the modern Narbonne), further along the coast to the west, was a Celtic town, as was Nyrax, which is thought to be the ancient city of Noreia in Austria. In the 5th century BC the Greek historian Herodotus reported that the Celts lived near the source of the river Danube and also beyond the Pillars of Hercules (the Straits of Gibraltar).

A century later, the Greek writer Ephoros described the Celts as one of the four great barbarian peoples, together with the Scythians, the Persians and the Libyans, who lived beyond the confines of the classical Mediterranean world. References to the islands of Albion and Ierne (Britain and Ireland) also date from the same period – in his famous voyage along the Atlantic coasts of western Europe in the 4th century BC, the explorer Pytheas of Massalia referred to them as the 'Pretannic Isles' that lay to the north of the lands of the Celts.

The origin of the term 'Keltoi' is unknown, although it is probably itself Celtic since it often appears in tribal names such as *Celtiberi*, and personal names such as *Celtillus*. In the 1st century BC, Julius Caesar wrote in the introduction to his *Commentaries on the Gallic War* (also translated as *The Conquest of Gaul*) that some of the tribes of Gaul referred to themselves collectively as Celts, 'although we [Romans]

Detail of the Gundestrup cauldron showing the head and arms of a deity flanked by two human figures. Note the torc and the horseman on the right who appears to interact with the larger figure. (Werner Forman Archive / National Museum, Copenhagen)

Hammered bronze disc from Ireland, 1st century AD. The main design is made up of several circles, varying in thickness and profile. The large boss is off-centre. Below it is perhaps an indication of a torc. (Werner Forman Archive / British Museum, London)

call them Gauls'. Writing two centuries later, the Greek author Pausanias remarked that *Keltoi* was believed to be a far older name than *Galli*. As to the meaning of these words, several explanations have been put forward. Based on Indo-European root words, 'noble' or 'exalted' has been suggested as a possible explanation for 'Celt', and 'strong' or 'powerful' for 'Gaul'. The term *Galli* was used by the Romans from the beginning of the 4th century BC to describe the Celts who invaded Italy, and later those who lived beyond the Alps in present-day France. The Greeks also used the name Galatoi, or Galatians, when referring to the Celtic-speaking peoples from central Europe who invaded Greece and later settled in Asia Minor (modern Turkey) in the 3rd century BC. The term 'Celtiberian' was used to describe the Celtic-speaking populations in the Iberian peninsula (Spain and Portugal), who were strongly influenced by the culture of the neighbouring Iberians. Today they are also referred to as Hispano-Celts. According to Pytheas, the inhabitants of Britain referred to themselves as *Pretani*.

The ancient Greeks described the *Keltoi* as living in what is now the Iberian peninsula, in France and in the upper reaches of the Danube valley in southern Germany. Over such a vast area, it is not possible to speak of a single Celtic people or race. They may have had much in common from the standpoint of material culture, social structure and religious belief, but the idea of a pan-European Celtic society and belief system, which was once widely held, is now seen as inaccurate and over-simplistic. Archaeological evidence indicates strong regional contrasts and variety suggesting a mosaic of diverse communities across Europe. One characteristic common to them all, however, was their language. Today, the most widely accepted definition of the Celts is based on language. Therefore, we can say that the Celts were those peoples living in central and western Europe in the latter half of the 1st millennium BC and speaking dialects of the family of languages now known as Celtic.

THE CELTIC LANGUAGES

The Celtic languages form part of the Indo-European language group. This group, which is one of the world's most extensive language groups, includes every modern European language except Basque, Estonian, Finnish and Hungarian, and also a number of languages that are now spoken in the Middle East and the Indian sub-continent, such as Iranian, Hindi and Urdu. Ancient Celtic can be divided into two broad groups: Continental and Insular. As the names imply, the former refers to the dialects spoken on mainland Europe, while the latter refers to those which were, and still are, spoken in the British Isles and also in Brittany. Whereas the Continental Celtic languages are now extinct, the Insular languages have survived and, although greatly changed, are one of our main sources of information about ancient Celtic society and its structure.

From the available evidence of place and personal names recorded on coins and inscriptions, it is possible to distinguish several different Continental Celtic dialects. In Iberia, Celtiberian was spoken across much of the central, northern and western peninsula. On the western seaboard and in the south-west, a separate dialect called

Celtic inscription written using the Greek alphabet, from Vaison-la-Romaine, France. (The Art Archive / Musée Lapidaire Avignon / Dagli Orti)

Lusitanian has also been identified. Gaulish was spoken over a wide area in what is now France and Belgium, and also across the Rhine valley. In the 1st century BC, Caesar remarked on the division of Gaul into three parts and referred to their inhabitants as *Belgae*, *Celtae* and *Aquitani*. The Romans continued to refer to them collectively as Gauls, but there is evidence from surviving Gaulish inscriptions to support the idea of differing dialects in Gaul. Gaulish inscriptions have also been found in northern Italy. However, in the area to the north-west of the Po valley and around the Italian lakes, an earlier form of Celtic has been detected, sometimes referred to as Lepontic. Inscriptions here pre-date the occupation of the Po valley by the Celts in the 4th century BC and present sufficient evidence to separate Lepontic from the Gaulish dialect introduced by the newcomers. In central Europe, a dense network of place names that differ from those found in the western Celtic dialects, and the known historical presence of Celtic-speaking peoples in the middle Danube region, are thought to indicate a further Celtic dialect. The language spoken by the Celtic migrants who settled in Asia Minor in the 3rd century BC was probably similar to this eastern Celtic dialect.

The Insular Celtic languages are divided into two branches: Brythonic, which was spoken in what is now England and Wales (where it remains a living language), and which was introduced into Brittany after the fall of the Roman Empire; and Goidelic, which is still spoken in Ireland, and which spread to Scotland and the Isle of Man in the post-Roman period. The language spoken by the ancient inhabitants of northern Britain, later known as the Picts, remains something of a mystery. Little is known about it, and the few surviving examples are limited to a handful of place and personal names and a few inscriptions that have defied translation. It has been suggested that Pictish is a pre-Celtic, non-Indo-European language, although those words that have been deciphered seem to be related to the Brythonic dialect.

The ancient Celtic languages are also sometimes divided into two further groups, commonly known as 'P-Celtic' and 'Q-Celtic'. The apparent difference is due to the replacement of what was assumed to be an earlier 'q' sound by a later 'p' sound. For instance, in Welsh, a Brythonic or P-Celtic language, the word for 'son' is *map*; the equivalent in Irish or Scots Gaelic, both Goidelic or Q-Celtic languages, is *mac*. Brythonic, Gaulish and Lepontic belong to the P-Celtic group, as does Galatian and so, presumably, does the eastern Celtic dialect. Goidelic, Celtiberian and Lusitanian belong to the Q-Celtic group. For many years, this difference was taken as clear evidence of 'the coming of the Celts' at various times to various places across Europe, particularly to the British Isles. Advances in archaeology and genetics have largely discredited this idea. The evolution of ancient European societies is now believed to be the result of the spread of ideas and cultural assimilation rather than successive waves of invaders. Instead of spreading out from one small region, it is thought that the Celtic languages evolved gradually over a wide area of Europe.

SOURCES OF EVIDENCE

Our knowledge of the ancient Celts and their world comes from a variety of sources. Unfortunately, these sources are usually fragmentary, often ambiguous and sometimes contradictory. They all have their shortcomings.

The accounts of Greek and Roman writers such as Herodotus, Polybius, Livy and Caesar provide the richest sources of information that we possess on the customs and history of the ancient Celts. They have the advantage of being closer in time to their subject, although rarely contemporary. Some merely draw their inspiration from others. They have to be read with caution since they generally

Lake Halstatt, the site of numerous rich finds from the early Iron Age. (akg-images / Erich Lessing)

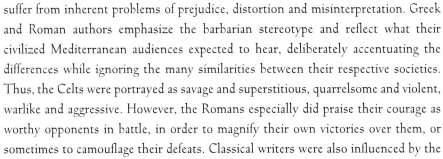

Halstatt warrior statue from the Hirschlanden burial, Württemberg, 6th century BC. (akg-images / Erich Lessing)

suffer from inherent problems of prejudice, distortion and misinterpretation. Greek and Roman authors emphasize the barbarian stereotype and reflect what their civilized Mediterranean audiences expected to hear, deliberately accentuating the differences while ignoring the many similarities between their respective societies. Thus, the Celts were portrayed as savage and superstitious, quarrelsome and violent, warlike and aggressive. However, the Romans especially did praise their courage as worthy opponents in battle, in order to magnify their own victories over them, or sometimes to camouflage their defeats. Classical writers were also influenced by the memories of the violent impact of the Celts on the Mediterranean world, especially the invasions of Italy and Greece. Their works provide a series of snapshots of the Celts and tend to represent Celtic society as static and unchanging, which was far from the case. Despite all this, without them our understanding of the Celts would be very different and much poorer.

The most tangible source of information comes from the study of the material remains of the Celts through modern archaeological excavation and analysis. Although on its own archaeology can only provide a partial picture, its great strength lies in the fact that it is free from the prejudice of classical commentators or mediaeval copyists (though not always from archaeologists themselves). A number of archaeologists have argued that since it is not known whether the peoples of Iron Age Europe, particularly those living in Britain and Ireland, identified themselves as Celts, it would not be accurate to refer to them as such. While it may be true that not all those peoples whom we now consider to be Celts considered themselves to be so, some of the peoples in Iron Age Europe did call themselves by this name. What is certain is that there was no Celtic 'ethnicity' or 'race' in ancient times, nor is there today. Recent genetic studies suggest that the population of Europe remained remarkably unchanged between the end of the last Ice Age, around 10,000 years ago, and the Migration Period at the end of the Roman Empire in the 4th and 5th centuries AD.

It used to be thought that the Celts were a completely non-literate society, but in recent years an increasing number of inscriptions in Celtic languages have been discovered, not all of which have been successfully translated. Depending on time and place, they are written in alphabets borrowed from Etruscan, Greek, Iberian or Latin. Other linguistic sources include place and personal names, Celtic words mentioned in classical texts and also the structure of modern Celtic languages. To these, we should also add the study of the vernacular literature of surviving Celtic societies in the post-Roman period. As with classical accounts, later vernacular sources must also be treated with caution.

A magnificent adorned disc of the early 4th century BC with coral inlays. (akg-images / Pietro Baguzzi)

They were written down for the first time almost a thousand years after the Celts had been conquered and absorbed into the Roman Empire. They were recorded by Christian monks in the early Middle Ages and, apart from the usual risk of bias, are all solely concerned with the myths and legends of Wales and Ireland, lands that lay at the very edge of the Celtic world in the pre-Roman period. We should not assume, therefore, that they can be used as models for Celtic societies in other parts of Europe. Although the linguistic evidence to support the existence of the Celts is complex and incomplete, it provides the clearest indication of an identifiable group of peoples in Iron Age Europe whom the Greeks and Romans referred to as Celts.

The various sources of evidence that we have at our disposal do reveal the existence of a major group of peoples in Iron Age Europe who spoke related languages and who shared similar beliefs, social structures, artistic styles and a pronounced taste for war. Such shared characteristics make it both logical and appropriate to refer to them by a common name. On their own, each of the sources can give only a limited view. When considered together, they enable us to compile a plausible, albeit generalized, picture of the Celts and their world.

CHRONOLOGY

BC

8th to 6th centuries	Early Iron Age Halstatt culture flourishes in west-central Europe.
c. 450	Decline of Halstatt Princedoms and expansion of La Tène Iron Age cultures. 'Keltoi' first mentioned by the Greeks.
c. 400	Beginning of 'Celtic migrations'. The Boii, Cenomani, Lingones and Senones settle in the Po valley and on the Adriatic coast. Other Celtic-speaking tribes move south-east along the Danube valley. Decline of Etruscan power in northern Italy.
387	Celts sack Rome.
335 and 323	Alexander the Great receives Celtic delegations in the Balkans and in Babylon.
281	Celts invade Macedonia. Victory over the Greeks at Thermopylae. The Celts go on to sack the sanctuary at Delphi but are defeated in battle (279). The survivors return to the Danube valley.
278	The Celtic Tectosages, Trocmii and Tolistobogii cross into Asia Minor.
275	Celtic Galatians defeated by Antiochus of Seleucia.
240	Galatians defeated by Attalus of Pergamon.
225	Celts defeated by Rome at Telamon. Decline of Celtic power in northern Italy, leading to the creation of the Roman province of Gallia Cisalpina.
218–202	Second Punic War. Celtiberian and Gallic mercenaries play a major role in Carthaginian victories over Rome.
197–179 and 154–133	Rome attempts to subdue the Celtiberian tribes in Iberia.
133	Celtiberian resistance broken at the siege of Numantia.
125	Rome intervenes on behalf of Massalia (Marseille) against the Gallic Saluvii. Beginning of Roman military intervention in Gaul.

124–121	Defeat of the Saluvii, Allobroges and Arverni by Rome. Foundation of the Roman military base at Aquae Sextiae (Aix-en-Provence).
118	Creation of the Roman province of Gallia Transalpina.
112–101	Migration of the Cimbri and Teutones, a mix of Celtic and Germanic peoples from northern Europe. After several victories over the Romans they are finally defeated by Marius at Aquae Sextiae in 102 and Vercellae in 101.
88–66	Galatians fight as allies of Rome in its war against Mithridates IV of Pontus.
64	Galatia becomes a client state of Rome. Deiotarus of the Tolistobogii becomes pre-eminent leader of the Galatians under the patronage of Pompey.
60	Celtic Boii and Scordisci defeated by Dacian tribes from the lower Danube.
58–51	Caesar's campaigns in Gaul, ending in the complete subjugation of the Gauls to Rome.
55 and 54	Reconnaissance in force by Caesar into south-eastern Britain.
52	Siege of Alésia. Surrender of Vercingetorix.

AD

43	Roman invasion of southern Britain. British resistance led by Caratacus until betrayed in 52 by Cartimandua, queen of the Brigantes.
60	Boudica's rebellion.
70s	Subjugation of northern Britain.
84	Agricola defeats the Caledones at the battle of Mons Graupius.
86–87	Roman withdrawal from southern Caledonia.
122	Hadrian visits Britain.
122–138	Construction of Hadrian's Wall and its associated forts.

Part 1
Out of the Mist

CHAPTER 1

THE RISE OF THE CELTIC WORLD

The Danube has its source in the land of the Celts near the city of Pyrene, and runs through the middle of Europe, dividing it into two portions. The Celts also live beyond the Pillars of Hercules and border on the Cynesiani, who are the westernmost of all the peoples of Europe. (Herodotus, Histories)

By the time they appear in the historical record in the 6th century BC, the Iron Age peoples called Celts by the ancient Greeks inhabited wide areas of central and western Europe, from the middle reaches of the Danube, across southern Germany, Austria, Switzerland, France and northern Italy to much of the Iberian peninsula. How they came to be there and from where they may have originated remain the subject of much debate. Neither the Greek authors who wrote the earliest accounts of the Celts, nor the Celts themselves have anything to say on the matter. The complete indifference of the former was expressed by the Roman historian Tacitus when he wrote that nobody bothered to enquire into the origins of barbarians. The latter, never having developed a fully literate culture, could not record their myths and legends, which as a result are lost to us. Archaeological evidence, however, shows that the Celts possessed a highly sophisticated material culture characterized by advanced metalworking skills and a distinctive style of decorative art.

PREVIOUS SPREAD
Bod da Loz, north of the Julier Pass in Switzerland, was a fortified settlement on one of the trade routes from the Mediterranean to the north during the Halstatt period. (akg-images / Erich Lessing)

BRONZE AND IRON

The formation of the Celtic world was a process that may be traced back to the cultures of the late Bronze Age. The European Bronze Age lasted from approximately 2500 to 800 BC. It was the period in which the production and use of metal tools and weapons first became widespread. Although knowledge of metalworking was known before this, with gold and copper being used to make cult objects and personal ornaments, it was the discovery of the much harder alloy bronze, produced by adding small amounts of tin or arsenic to copper during the smelting process, that made the replacement of flint and other stone implements a practical proposition. Both copper and tin are relatively rare in Europe and are found in only a small number of locations compared with flint, which is far more common. The adoption of bronze technology brought about an increase in long-distance trade across the continent as communities that previously had been largely self-sufficient endeavoured to gain access to these precious metals. Increased trading links facilitated the exchange of ideas and artistic styles, which in turn encouraged greater cultural uniformity.

By the late Bronze Age, in the period from 1300 to 800 BC, the Urnfield culture had become one of the most important in Europe. It is so-called because of its distinctive burial practice in which the dead were cremated and their ashes placed in ceramic funerary urns for interment in vast flat cemeteries. The Urnfield culture spread across Europe from the Hungarian plain to eastern France and from Poland to northern Italy following the decline of the Mycenaean–Minoan civilization in the Aegean region, which provoked extensive social and economic change in central Europe. In the Urnfield zone, the principal east–west trade routes, linking the Black Sea with the Atlantic, crossed those from north to south between the Baltic and the Mediterranean. Control of trade and the production of bronze implements led to the emergence of a social elite in late Bronze Age Urnfield societies, which became progressively more hierarchical, prefiguring the type of aristocratic society that characterized the Celts of the Iron Age. At one time, the spread of the Urnfield culture was thought to be an indication of the expansion of the Celts from a hypothetical homeland in central Europe. However, no archaeological evidence has been found to support the large-scale movement of peoples during this period, and the theory has now been discarded.

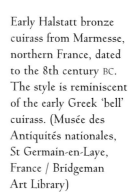

Early Halstatt bronze cuirass from Marmesse, northern France, dated to the 8th century BC. The style is reminiscent of the early Greek 'bell' cuirass. (Musée des Antiquités nationales, St Germain-en-Laye, France / Bridgeman Art Library)

Detail of a Halstatt warrior statue from the Glauburg burial, Hesse, 5th century BC. The armour is reminiscent of Greek or Etruscan styles. (akg-images)

From the beginning of the 1st millennium BC, iron began to replace bronze as the metal of choice for the manufacture of tools and weapons. Iron ore is far more common in Europe than the ingredients of bronze and once forged is harder and will retain a much better cutting edge. First introduced into Greece from Asia Minor about 1200 BC, ironworking quickly spread westwards across the Mediterranean basin and along the Danube valley. By about 800 BC the change from bronze to iron technology was complete in central and southern Europe, although it would take another two centuries or more to reach Britain, Iberia and Scandinavia.

The European Iron Age is traditionally divided into two phases, each named after a particular archaeological site where the characteristics of each were first recognized. The earlier, or Halstatt, period has been accepted as the earliest material culture specific to the Celts. It first emerged within the Urnfield zone in southern Germany, Austria and Bohemia, but only developed a distinctive character of its own with the transition from the late Bronze to the early Iron Age, when it spread to much of western Europe including France, Switzerland, the Low Countries, and as far as south-east Britain and parts of the Iberian peninsula. Just as with the Urnfield culture, the spread of the Halstatt culture, although it can be clearly identified as Celtic, does not imply the 'coming of the Celts'. It was rather the result of trade and social contact between peoples who shared similar values and who spoke similar languages. Even so, Halstatt and Celtic are not synonymous. Some Celtic-speaking regions, Iberia in particular, only partially adopted the Halstatt culture, while others, such as Ireland, did not adopt it at all.

The Halstatt culture is named after the site in the Austrian Alps where excavations in the mid-19th century brought to light a large number of rich burials. Living close to a major trade route between central Europe and the Mediterranean, this community had grown wealthy on the profits of the trade in rock salt, another prized commodity essential in the preservation of food. Many of the burial sites contained rich funerary offerings that revealed a society ruled by an aristocratic elite and included long iron swords that were recognized as being similar to those described in ancient Greek accounts of the *Keltoi*.

Major changes followed the introduction of iron technology, intensifying the trends that had begun in the late Bronze Age. In the central Halstatt zone, there was a marked increase in the

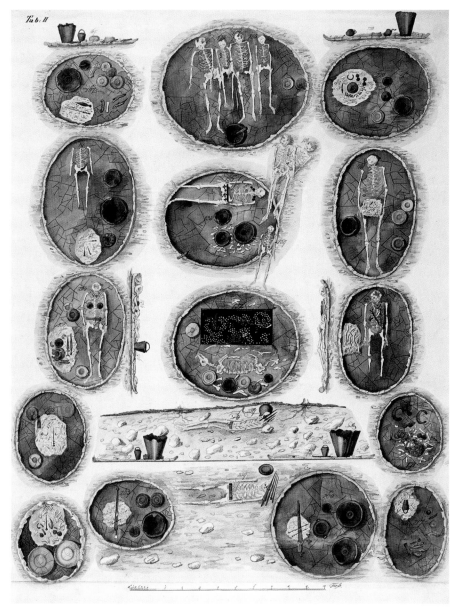

Colour lithograph based on the notes of Johann Georg Ramsauer on some of the graves he excavated at Halstatt, 1846–63. By the standards of the time, the recording of the excavations was extremely meticulous. (akg-images / Erich Lessing)

number of hillforts, large fortified hilltop sites often enclosed by an intricate system of earth banks and ditches. A change in burial practice from cremation, typical of the Urnfield culture, to individual inhumation suggests the adoption of new belief systems. Rich grave goods reveal the development of a reinforced social hierarchy and the continuing emergence of a dominant elite. One type of artefact discovered in many Halstatt burials that provides a clear indication of an elite social group is

Detail of the Halstatt scabbard showing warriors carrying spears and shields, 6th century BC. (akg-images / Erich Lessing)

horse gear. From the 8th century BC onwards, the graves of the Halstatt aristocracy are characterized by four-wheeled vehicles together with bits and other items of horse harness, as well as long slashing swords representative of the aristocratic warrior. Horse trappings and four-wheeled wagons are common in burial rites in eastern Europe and on the Eurasian steppe beyond. The growing importance of the horse and the ceremonial wagon as status symbols for the Halstatt chiefdoms, with the implied emphasis on cavalry in war, has been linked to the influence of the Indo-Iranian peoples known to the classical Greek authors as Cimmerians or Scythians. Groups of these mounted nomads moved west from the Pontic steppe north of the Black Sea to settle in the Hungarian plain. Contact between them and the Halstatt communities in Austria, Bohemia and southern Germany introduced new and exotic customs for the ruling elite to display and reinforce their status.

MEDITERRANEAN POWER POLITICS

To better understand the changes that were taking place in temperate Europe at this time, we must also look at what was happening around the Mediterranean, since the two worlds would from now on become increasingly bound together. The 8th century BC was particularly important for the Mediterranean world. It was at this time that the earliest Greek colonies were founded, and the Phoenician trading system developed. Greek adventurers began to explore and exploit the rich mineral resources around the west coast of Italy and the islands of Elba, Corsica and Sardinia. Later Greek settlement in Sicily and southern Italy itself was so extensive that the entire area became known as Magna Graecia, 'Greater Greece'.

The introduction of exotic goods and ideas from the eastern Mediterranean in exchange for metals and other raw materials acted as a stimulus on the indigenous cultures of the region, in particular on the Etruscans. Long considered one of the 'mysterious' peoples of ancient European history, the Etruscans had their origins in the Villanovan culture of late Bronze Age Italy. Much of what we know about them comes from Roman sources. In its early history, Rome was subject to Etruscan domination; its point of view, therefore, is inevitably hostile and prejudiced. The Etruscans' own language is non-Indo-European and has not been successfully deciphered. It is not possible, therefore, for them to give us their own version of events. The mystery surrounding Etruscan origins – that they perhaps arrived in Italy from Asia Minor or from elsewhere in the eastern Mediterranean at some unspecified time in the ancient past – can be explained by recognizing the impact of

Detail of the bronze embossed vessel known as the Benvenuti Situla showing Etruscan chariot and warrior, 7th century BC. (The Art Archive / Museo Nazionale Atestino Este / Dagli Orti)

Bronze statuette of a warrior from Liechtenstein dated to the 5th century BC. Note the Greek/Etruscan-style cuirass. (akg-images / Erich Lessing)

external influences on the indigenous Bronze Age culture introduced as a result of the expansion of Greek and Phoenician trade in the western Mediterranean. The introduction of prestige goods encouraged the rapid development of Etruscan society, with the aristocratic elite controlling the flow of trade. Within a hundred years, Etruscan coastal cities had developed commercial interests of their own and had begun to venture out along the coasts of Gaul and Iberia.

In parallel with Greek expansion around and beyond the Italian peninsula, the Phoenicians, from the two great cities of Tyre and Sidon, on the coast of modern Lebanon, were establishing trading enclaves along the North African coastline as far as the Atlantic. The port of Gadir, modern Cadiz, is said to date back as early as 1100 BC, while the foundation of the greatest Phoenician city in the western Mediterranean, Carthage, is traditionally set at about 814 BC. Like their Greek rivals, the Phoenicians went out in search of metals and raw materials. In southern Iberia they found silver and copper in abundance, where the almost mythical realm of Tartessos, the 'Tarshish' of the Bible, owed its fame to the mineral riches of the Rio Tinto and Sierra Morena. The quantity of silver exported via Gadir became legendary throughout the ancient Mediterranean world. From this base, Phoenician traders began to explore the coastlines of the Atlantic to the north and south, drawn by the prospect of further mineral wealth, and are said to have traded for tin in Cornwall. Carthage became the centre of Phoenician power in the western Mediterranean, with the foundation of further settlements and trading enclaves in western Sicily, Sardinia and the Balearic islands.

In the mid-6th century BC, the Greek cities on the coast of Asia Minor were threatened by the growing power of the Persian Empire. The Phocaeans had founded their colony of Massalia, modern Marseille, in 600 BC, and went on to establish settlements at Emporion, modern Ampurias, on the Spanish Costa Brava, and at Alalia in Corsica. Faced now with the Persian threat, they decided to abandon their home city of Phocis and emigrate en masse to Alalia. The Etruscan cities made an alliance with Carthage against the Greek interlopers. The great naval battle that took place off Alalia in 537 BC was a victory for the Greeks who, nevertheless, decided to move to a more secure area on the southern Italian mainland.

The battle of Alalia was a major turning point in the history of the western Mediterranean. Following their defeat, the Etruscan coastal cities

Miniature bronze cult wagon from the Halstatt period, 7th century BC. (akg-images / Erich Lessing)

lost much of their power. Etruscan city states inland began to develop new trade routes across the Apennines to the Po valley and the Adriatic coast. New markets were opened up to the north across the Alps via the Celtic-speaking Golaseccan culture. While Carthage continued to dominate southern Iberia and the Atlantic sea lanes, victory at Alalia left the Greeks of Massalia in control of the main trade routes that led northward via the Rhône–Saône valley into the heart of western Europe. For the first time, the Iron Age communities there came into direct contact with the Mediterranean world.

THE HALSTATT PRINCEDOMS

The shift in the balance of power in the western Mediterranean that followed the Greek victory at the battle of Alalia had a significant impact on the Halstatt communities of transalpine Europe. In the 6th century BC there was a marked increase in the level of contact and interaction between the Mediterranean world, transalpine Europe and the Atlantic coasts to the north-west. The main reason for this was Europe's mineral wealth, particularly in tin, which was essential for production of the bronze that was still preferred by metalworkers, despite the increasing use of iron.

The intensification of Greek-led trade passing through Massalia encouraged a corresponding shift in the focus of power among the Halstatt chiefdoms. This was now centred on a region stretching from Burgundy in France to southern Germany, to the north and north-east of the corridor formed by the rivers Rhône and Saône. Among the most important centres of power were Mont Lassois, near the source of the river Seine in France, and the Heuneburg, on the upper Danube in south-west Germany. Archaeological evidence indicates rapid social change, particularly in those areas where the flow of trade could be channelled and thus controlled. Power was becoming more concentrated: hillforts became fewer in number but more massive in size. The number of elite burials also fell, but those which have survived

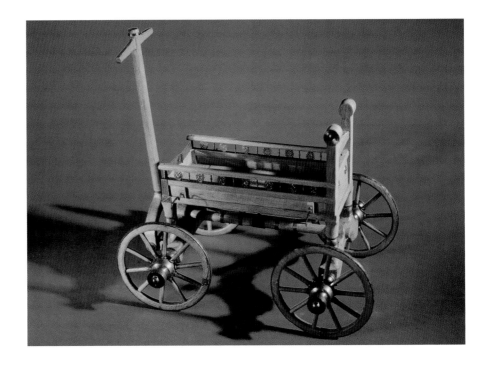

Model of the wagon from the tomb of the Vix Princess. (The Art Archive / Museum Châtillon-sur-Seine / Dagli Orti)

intact display extraordinary riches. The term 'Halstatt Princedoms' has been coined to describe these communities whose elites were able to control the flow of the exotic Mediterranean products that were so avidly sought in order to enhance and display their status. These 'Halstatt Princes' have been compared to the legendary kings of Ireland. Their elaborate funerary practices have striking parallels with those of the Etruscans, with whom there was also increasing contact via the Alps.

One of the most important elements of these 'princely' burials was the four-wheeled wagon on which the body of the deceased was laid and brought to his tomb. According to Herodotus, the royal burials of the Scythians presented many similarities. Bronze drinking vessels of Mediterranean origin are another clear

The Vix krater. A bronze vessel intended for the mixing of wine, it is the largest example ever found: 1.64m tall, with a capacity of over 1,000 litres. (akg-images / Archives CDA / Guillo)

Detail of the Vix torc, one of the treasures of early Celtic art. (akg-images / Erich Lessing)

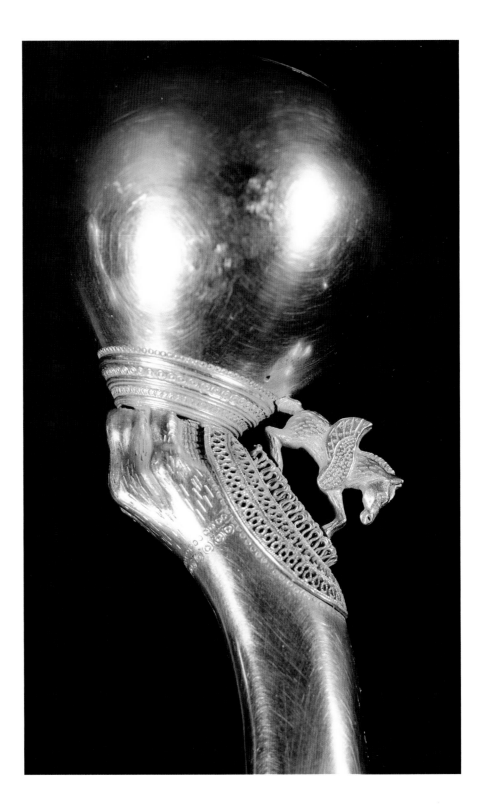

indication of elite status. A great many of the Greek and Etruscan luxury goods imported into transalpine Europe at this time were linked to the transportation, preparation and consumption of wine. Later sources tell us how wine was much sought after by the Celtic nobility. Vines had not yet been introduced north of the Alps. The customs connected with the *symposion*, the ritual wine-drinking ceremony of the Greeks, were swiftly adopted by the Halstatt Princes and adapted to their own tradition of ceremonial consumption of alcohol similar to those described in Irish texts. Two of the most spectacular examples of the wealth and status enjoyed by the Halstatt elite are the tombs discovered at Vix, near the hillfort of Mont Lassois in Burgundy, and at Hochdorf, in Baden-Württemberg.

THE VIX PRINCESS

The excavation of an early Iron Age cemetery at Vix in 1953 revealed the tomb of a woman who was aged about 35 years old, dating from the end of the 6th century BC. Clearly indicating high status among the Halstatt elite, the tomb of the 'Vix Princess', as this woman has become known, is rightly regarded as one of the treasures of the early Celtic period. Her body lay on the chassis of a finely worked four-wheeled wagon that had been used as a bier. Around her neck was a beautiful gold torc, or neck ring, weighing almost 0.5kg (1.1lb); other gold items lay around her. The burial chamber contained a bronze Etruscan wine flagon and Greek drinking cups, and the tomb was dominated by an enormous bronze *krater*, or wine-mixing vessel (see p.27). An astonishing 1.64m (5ft 4in) tall, it had a capacity of 1,100 litres (241 gallons). It was decorated with figures representing Greek warriors and chariots, and was surmounted by a lid featuring a figurine of a young woman. From its artistic style, it is believed to have been made in Sparta or perhaps in one of the Greek cities of southern Italy. Weighing over 200kg (440lb), it is likely to have been transported in pieces and reassembled at its destination.

Gold shoe fittings from the tomb of the Hochdorf Prince. (Landesmuseum Württemberg Stuttgart; P. Frankenstein, H. Zwietasch)

Several other female 'princely' burials have been discovered dating from the end of the 6th and beginning of the 5th centuries BC, although none compare with that of the Vix Princess. Though far from common, they do give us an indication of the high status of some women in early Celtic society.

THE HOCHDORF PRINCE

In 1977, an amateur archaeologist discovered traces of a burial site at Hochdorf in south-west Germany. Excavations revealed a wooden burial chamber in a pit 2.4m (7ft 10in) deep that had been surrounded by an outer chamber built of massive beams and boulders. It had been covered originally by a huge earth mound some 60m (196ft 10in) across and 6m (19ft 8in) high. Like the burial of the Vix Princess, it is believed to date from the end of the 6th century BC. The tomb contained the body of a man about 40 years old, 1.87m (6ft 1in) tall and strongly built. He lay on a remarkable bronze couch, 3m (9ft 10in) long that was decorated with figures and vehicles made by punching a dotted outline in the bronze sheet. Traces of fabric showed that it had been upholstered. This Halstatt Prince wore an arm ring, a torc and a belt made of gold. Even his footwear had very thin gold plaques. These show that his ankle-length boots had slightly curved toes, in a style that is known from Etruscan wall paintings and also from the engraved figures on an early La Tène sword scabbard. Beside the body on the couch had stood a four-wheeled wagon originally encased in thin plates of bronze and iron. Nine bronze dishes, nine drinking horns and a large bronze cauldron from Italy are reminiscent of the Greek *symposion*, in which nine was the ideal number of participants. The tomb also contained evidence of hunting in the form of fish hooks and arrowheads, together with a horse harness, an iron axe and a spear. Although it is clear from the wealth of the grave goods and the care with which the tomb was prepared that the Hochdorf Prince was a powerful member of the Halstatt aristocracy, he does not appear to have been a warrior.

The Hochdorf cauldron. (Landesmuseum Württemberg Stuttgart; P. Frankenstein, H. Zwietasch)

Not far from Hochdorf, the Heuneberg hillfort dominated the trade routes that crossed the upper Danube nearby. One of the principal centres of Halstatt power, the site was inhabited from the 7th to the late 5th century BC, until it was finally destroyed by fire. For a time, the Heuneberg presented a unique appearance among Iron Age hillforts in transalpine Europe. During the 6th century BC, parts of its ramparts were rebuilt with sun-dried bricks in a style remarkably like the

walls of contemporary Greek fortresses, complete with bastion towers. It is one of the clearest indications that we have of the influence of ideas from the Mediterranean on the Halstatt world. However, this particular example was to prove relatively short-lived. Whoever organized the construction of the wall failed completely to take into account the climate of central Europe: mudbrick soon dissolves in the rain. The Heuneberg's rampart was very soon repaired in the traditional Celtic manner using wooden beams and stone. Just like other major hillforts at this time, the Heuneberg had a number of elite graves close by. Sadly, many of these were looted for their treasures long ago. One, though, was discovered intact, containing the remains of another woman of high status and the earliest traces of silk to be found in Europe.

Imported luxury items are almost unknown beyond the immediate area of the Halstatt hillforts and the richest of the surrounding elite burials. The concentration of power that gave rise to large fortified centres such as Mont Lassois and the Heuneberg in the 6th century BC suggests that trade for Greek and Etruscan prestige goods and their distribution within Halstatt society were controlled by a very small number of people: the Halstatt Princes and their entourage.

Bronze couch from the tomb of the Hochdorf Prince. (Landesmuseum Württemberg Stuttgart; P. Frankenstein, H. Zwietasch)

THE EMERGENCE OF THE HISTORICAL CELTS AND THE BIRTH OF LA TÈNE CIVILIZATION

The Halstatt Princedoms collapsed during the first half of the 5th century BC. Centres of power such as Mont Lassois and the Heuneberg were abandoned, the latter perhaps as a result of a violent attack. The causes of this sudden decline are unclear. Several factors have been put forward to try to explain it: internal social pressures linked to changing trading patterns, climate change, and in particular the impact of the rise of warrior societies to the north.

Shortly after 500 BC, trade between Massalia and the Halstatt centres of power seems to have come to an almost complete halt. Contact between transalpine Europe and the Mediterranean world was now redirected over the Alps via the territory of the Golaseccan Celts and the new Etruscan settlements in the Po valley, and also via the Greek trading ports of Adria and Spina at the head of the Adriatic. Mediterranean luxury goods are now found beyond the Halstatt zone, in elite graves around the confluence of the Rhine and Moselle rivers in western Germany, and in the Marne–Champagne area of north-eastern France. Similarly rich graves have also been found further east, in Austria and Bohemia. The principal difference between these and the rich cemeteries of the Halstatt Princes is their military aspect. The deceased is accompanied by his personal weapons: spear, javelins and shield for the most part, occasionally a sword. Some contain the remains of a two-wheeled chariot, which replaced the four-wheeled wagon in Halstatt elite burials. Prestige items imported from the Mediterranean were still largely associated with wine-drinking but were to have a major influence on the evolution of the material culture of the later Iron Age communities of Europe. The decorative motifs on Etruscan bronzes, with their exotic oriental influences, inspired craftsmen and artisans to emulate and adapt these styles, moving away from the typical geometric style of the Halstatt period. This new material culture and artistic style is known as La Tène, and is characteristic of the Celts as they now begin to enter the historical record.

The La Tène culture is named after a site at Lake Neuchâtel in Switzerland. Excavations in the latter part of the 19th century revealed a series of ancient timber

Iron dagger with gold-plated hilt and sheath from a Halstatt tomb, mid-5th century BC. Note the sun-wheel symbols that form the 'antenna'-type hilt. (akg-images / Erich Lessing)

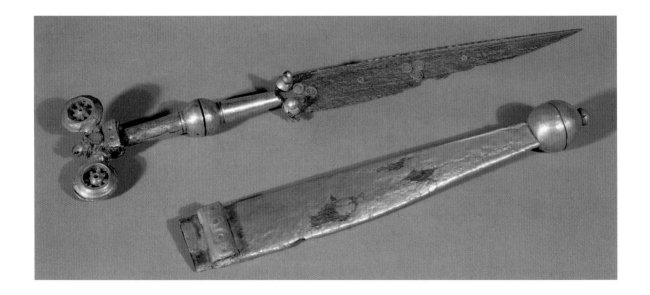

piles driven into the bed of the lake, which are now believed to be the remains of two bridges crossing the river Thielle. Further discoveries included human remains, several hundred swords and spearheads, together with other items such as bronze brooches and cauldrons, and iron tools and ingots. The waterlogged nature of the site preserved not only the timbers of the bridges but also a number of other wooden artefacts, including yokes and shields which would otherwise have completely decayed and been lost. Thanks to this, one of the bridges has been dated to the mid-3rd century BC. The nature of the site at La Tène is still the subject of debate. It is fairly certain that it was a religious site where offerings to the gods were cast into the lake. However, it is possible that it was also a trading post connected to a settlement that was abandoned after persistent flooding.

The later Iron Age culture known as La Tène is defined by its distinctive curvilinear (curving line) art style, which was born out of a synthesis of traditional Halstatt geometrical and Greek and Etruscan vegetal decorative forms, derived from imported drinking vessels. It can be seen at its finest on weapons and other items of luxury metalwork. The source of inspiration for many early aspects of La Tène culture can be found in Italy. Ceramics and jewellery are recognizably Italian in style, modelled on Etruscan originals. Even the two-wheeled chariot that replaced the four-wheeled ceremonial wagon of the Halstatt culture in funerary rites, and which is often seen as typical of Celtic warfare, is thought to be inspired by Etruscan models. The Celtic sword, the weapon that was to characterize the Celtic warrior for centuries to come, and which would cause such terror in the Mediterranean world, was also developed at this time. During the 5th century BC, swords were carried by a relatively small number of warriors. They appear in only about 20 per cent of elite graves in the Marne–Champagne region, and even less further east in the Rhineland. The spear or javelin was still the most widely used offensive weapon of the warrior.

Like the culture of the Halstatt Celts before it, the main elements of the new La Tène culture developed among a minority of the Celtic peoples of Europe, and were similarly restricted to the social elite. From the second half of the 5th century BC, it spread outwards to become the dominant culture across transalpine Europe from the Atlantic coast of France to the Carpathian basin. Its influence was felt in Spain and northern Italy, and by the 1st century BC had reached the British Isles. However, it would be wrong to assume that economic contact with the Mediterranean world was the prime cause of change in transalpine Europe. The formation of Celtic Europe was a process that began long before the Celts emerged into recorded history in the 6th century BC. It involved Celtic-speaking cultures dating back to the late Bronze Age and early Iron Age. Many of the characteristics of Iron Age Celtic society have

Gold Schwarzenbach
cup from an elite grave in
Germany, 5th century BC.
(bpk / Antikensammlung
Staatliche Museen
zu Berlin, photo
Ingrid Geske)

clear precedents in the Bronze Age, in particular the concentration of power. The
import of exotic luxury items accentuated an already existing trend towards
increased social stratification among Celtic-speaking communities, accelerating the
development of centralized chiefdoms and the formation of an elite class which
controlled and monopolized the flow of trade. In some parts of the early Celtic
world, such as Bohemia, there is very little evidence of imported Mediterranean
prestige goods. Yet the development of the large fortified settlement at Závist (near
Prague) during the 6th century BC suggests that more complex societies were also
evolving in response to internal pressures.

Whatever the reasons behind the rapid decline of the Halstatt Princedoms and
the rise of the La Tène warrior societies in the mid-5th century BC, it is clear that
this was a period of considerable upheaval in certain areas of transalpine Europe.
Within a couple of generations, large numbers of people began to leave their homes
and move south towards Italy. The Celts were about to emerge out of the mist and
into the glare of the Mediterranean sun. To the Greeks and Etruscans, the Celts
would cease to be the strange, distant barbarians who would trade almost anything
for wine. From now on the Celts would be a reality that was terrifyingly close.

CHAPTER 2

MIGRANTS AND MERCENARIES

They are wont to change their abode on the slightest provocation, migrating in bands
with all their battle array, or setting out with their entire households when displaced
by a stronger enemy. (Strabo, Geography)

All the evidence that we possess indicates that large-scale movements of Celtic-speaking peoples occurred on a number of occasions in the later Iron Age. Over the last few years, developments in archaeology and genetic studies have cast new light on these movements, provoking renewed debate on their extent and significance, particularly concerning the British Isles. Migration was one of the most effective ways of relieving internal tensions caused by the increase in population that occurred in some areas of central and western Europe towards the end of the Halstatt period. Similar problems of overpopulation and the consequent drain on limited resources had been experienced by the Greek city states in the Aegean region some 200 years earlier in the 7th century BC. They had been resolved by sending out groups of emigrants to found colonies around the Mediterranean and Black Sea coasts. One of the most important was Massalia, which had a major influence on the early Celtic Halstatt Princedoms.

'ENEMY AT THE GATES' – THE CELTIC INVASION OF ITALY

In writing about the migration of Celtic tribes to Italy, the Roman historian Livy said that the Celts of Gaul were under the domination of the powerful tribe known as the Bituriges. At that time, their king was Ambigatus, under whose rule Gaul had grown

The Celtic migrations
of the 4th and 3rd
centuries BC.

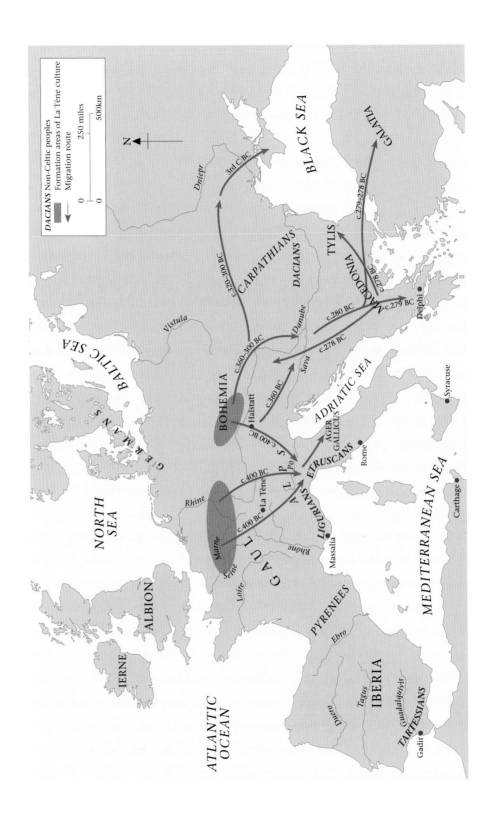

so wealthy and populous that it was becoming extremely difficult to govern. The aging king determined to send his nephews, Bellovesus and Segovesus, to find new homes 'as the gods might assign them'. Reading between the lines, we might interpret this as an attempt to remove two particularly aggressive elements from the court and prevent them from disputing the succession. One of the principal characteristics of Celtic society was the constant competition for power and status among the members of the noble elite. Segovesus was assigned the Hercynian highlands: Bohemia and the Harz mountains. Bellovesus was favoured with 'a far pleasanter road': Italy. Accompanied by not only the surplus population of the Bituriges, but also that of various subject tribes – the Arverni, Senones, Aedui, Ambarri, Carnutes and Aulerci – Bellovesus set off with an army of vast numbers of infantry and cavalry.

The arrival of large numbers of Celts from transalpine Europe in Italy at the end of the 5th and beginning of the 4th centuries BC is the first certain event that we know of in Celtic history. Livy's account suggests that the principal reason was overpopulation, an opinion supported by Plutarch and Pompeius Trogus, who was himself a Celt. The rapid decline of the Halstatt Princedoms and the rise of the La Tène warrior societies caused considerable social and economic unrest. Migration was certainly a practical solution to the problems caused by excess population and internal conflict. Exactly where these Celtic migrants came from remains unclear. It is possible that they originated from the Marne–Moselle area of northern France, where the La Tène culture largely developed. However, the tribes mentioned by Livy are known to have lived further south, along the line of the rivers Seine and Loire. The close trading links that had developed between transalpine Europe and Italy in the 5th century BC were a major factor in the Celtic migrations a century later. Those areas where trade was most intense were those that experienced the greatest movement of population: three-quarters of the burial sites in the densely populated Marne area were apparently abandoned in a fairly short space of time. A similar phenomenon can also be seen in Bohemia. It seems likely, therefore, that the greater part of the migrants came from these two broad areas. Further clues of their geographical origins can be found in the names of the most important tribes involved. The Senones and the Cenomani are recorded in both northern France and Italy; the Boii came from Bohemia, from which tribe the region takes its name. Nevertheless, the movement of Celtic peoples at this time was so widespread that it is quite possible that it affected most of the La Tène region.

Classical accounts of the Celtic migrations to Italy are confirmed by archaeology. Excavations have revealed a sudden influx of La Tène artefacts into Italy across the

Detail from an Etruscan urn showing Etruscans and Gauls fighting. (akg-images / Rabatti – Domingie)

Po valley from the Alps to the Apennines except for the territory of the native Celts of the Golaseccan culture. The impact is particularly evident in the distribution of La Tène swords. Whereas only a few examples from the 5th century BC have been found in the foothills of the Alps, the characteristic shapes of blades dating from the 4th and 3rd centuries BC have been found throughout this area as well as in neighbouring regions, especially Etruria and further south. It is highly likely that this was due to the presence of Celtic mercenaries. Another major indication of migration is the jewellery of high-status Celtic women. Jewellery found in burials of female Italian Senones is similar to that worn in Champagne in the 5th century BC, but unlike that of any others in Italy. Burial rites themselves also provide valuable information. The Boii were the only Celtic migrants in Italy to continue to practise cremation just as they had done in Bohemia.

The migrants from Gaul and Bohemia were not the first Celtic-speaking peoples in Italy. Inscriptions dating from the 6th century BC, the oldest known inscriptions in any Celtic language, indicate that a distinctive form of Celtic, sometimes known as Lepontic (see p.10), was already spoken at that time in the area of the Italian lakes in the foothills of the Alps. This area coincides with that of the Golaseccan culture, which is thought to have originated about 1000 BC and is now associated with the Insubres, one of the main Celtic peoples of the Po valley in historical times.

The Celtic migrations to Italy did not simply happen. They seem to have been carefully planned and organized by the tribal elites, almost certainly in collaboration with, on the one hand, the Golaseccan Celts and, on the other, the Greeks of the powerful city state of Syracuse in Sicily. One of the motives of the former was perhaps to counter the growing influence of the Etruscans who were consolidating their position in the Po valley, while the latter sought to extend their control north along the Adriatic coast. In describing the intended migration of the Helvetii, a Celtic tribe living in modern Switzerland in the 1st century BC, Julius Caesar wrote that they spent two years preparing for the journey, building up food stocks, wagons and draft animals, and negotiating with other tribes whose territory they would have to cross in order to reach their destination on the far side of Gaul. While the Insubres remained in their traditional homelands in the foothills of the Alps and in Piedmont, concentrated around their capital Mediolanum (Milan), the three principal groups of Celtic migrants moved further south and south-east into the Italian peninsula. The Cenomani settled around Brescia and Verona, between the Insubres and the non-Celtic Veneti, forcing the Boii to cross the Po in search of land

Early La Tène wagon made from bronze and wood, discovered in an elite grave in Lombardy, northern Italy. (akg-images / Pietro Baguzzi)

to settle. Their invasion of Etruscan and Umbrian territory between the Po and the Apennine mountains met with substantial resistance. Near the Etruscan city of Felsina (Bologna), scenes of battle with Celtic warriors have been found on a number of Etruscan burial *stelae* that date from the late 5th century BC. The Senones settled further south still along the Adriatic coast, from Ariminum to the river Aso, in such numbers that the region became known as the *ager gallicus*, 'the country of the Gauls'. Here they could dominate the valley of the Tiber, the key to central Italy, and threaten the Greek cities in Apuglia and Campania. So numerous were the Celts who settled in the Po valley and beyond, that the Romans named the area Gallia Cisalpina, 'Gaul on this side of the Alps'.

THE SACK OF ROME, 387 BC

At the time when Dionysius of Syracuse was besieging Rhegium [391 BC], the Celts who lived in the regions beyond the Alps streamed through the passes in great strength and seized the territory that lay between the Apennine mountains and the Alps, expelling the Etruscans who lived there. (Diodorus Siculus, *Historical Library*)

By 400 BC, vast numbers of Celts had crossed the Alps into Italy to settle in the Po valley and along the northern Adriatic coast. The Etruscan cities whose territories they raided appealed for help from their neighbours. In 387 BC, the Senones, led by a chieftain named Brennus (the Raven), laid siege to the Etruscan city of Clusium. Ambassadors from Rome were sent at the request of the Etruscans to attempt to mediate between the warring parties. However, in breech of custom the Roman delegation sided with the Etruscans and took up arms against the Celts, who were outraged at this disregard for the international law of the time. Leaving part of his force to continue the siege of Clusium, Brennus immediately marched on Rome, inflicting a crushing defeat on the Roman army on the river Allia, some 15km (9 miles) north of the city. The date of the battle, 18 July, was forever after considered a day of ill omen in Rome. While the survivors took refuge in nearby Veii, the Celts went on to sack Rome itself. According to legend, the Capitol alone held out, withstanding surprise attacks at night thanks to the cackling of the sacred geese. In the end, the Gauls, as they were known by the Romans, had to be bought off after an occupation of seven months on payment of one hundred pounds of gold, plus the weight of Brennus' sword, which he is traditionally said to have thrown on the scales with the contemptuous cry of 'Vae Victis!' ('Woe to the conquered!') in response to Roman complaints that they were fixed.

Bronze Italo-Celtic
helmet with elaborate
crest fitting for plumes
or feathers, mid-4th
century BC. (akg-images)

News of the fall of Rome quickly spread. Contemporary Greek writers noted that an army of Hyperboreans (barbarians from the north) had taken a Greek city called Rome far away near the 'great sea' (the Mediterranean). This defeat and humiliation at the hands of the Celts had a profound and long-lasting effect on the Romans. From that moment on, the Gauls were regarded with fear and loathing, a permanent threat from the north, the *terror gallicus*. It was used to justify all manner of actions in revenge and continued to shape Roman attitudes to the Gauls for centuries after.

The arrival of the Celts in Italy did not result in the expulsion of the native populations. Despite their numbers, the Celts were still a minority. Archaeological evidence points to a considerable degree of cultural exchange and assimilation, especially between the local and Celtic elites. Although in the north the Cenomani tended to preserve a more distinct La Tène culture, further south the Boii and the Senones were more influenced by their Etruscan neighbours. Unlike the Celts elsewhere in Europe at this time, many Italian Celts lived in settlements large enough to be considered towns. The Insubres of northern Italy were already urbanized at the time of the Celtic migration, and Etruscan cities such as Felsina became important centres of Celtic population. The majority, however, continued to live in a similar rural environment to that which they had known in their homelands. The Roman writer Livy described the Boii living in small farms and hilltop villages. Recent excavations at Monte Bibele in the Apennine mountains have revealed evidence of Celtic rural life in Italy: graves in the cemetery there show a gradual progression from purely Etruscan to a mix of Etruscan and Celtic burials over a period of 200 years in the 4th and 3rd centuries BC. The level of integration between the native and immigrant communities was such that the culture of the Boii and the Senones at this time has been termed 'Italo-Celtic'. Only the characteristic La Tène sword, the symbol of the Celtic warrior, remained unaffected by local artistic styles. It was adopted by many, including the Ligurian peoples of the Alps and Mediterranean coast of northern Italy, the Umbrian hill people of the Apennines and the Veneti at the head of the Adriatic, all of them non-Celtic peoples. Because of this, it is often difficult to differentiate between ethnic origins, which have to be determined in other ways such as the type of burial rite. The predominance of the La Tène sword throughout many parts of Italy as a weapon of choice is a clear indication of the prowess of the Celtic military elite and the reputation of Celtic mercenary warriors.

The Celts in Italy were by no means united. The Boii were the traditional allies of the Insubres, whereas the Cenomani tended to side with the Veneti and often the Romans in order to preserve their independence. The Senones were allied with the Syracusans and probably provided Dionysius of Syracuse with the first Celtic mercenaries who are explicitly mentioned in ancient sources as part of a force sent from Sicily against the Thebans in Greece in 369–368 BC. Although their origins are not specified, it is likely that they were recruited from Italy via the Syracusan trading port of Ancona near the lands occupied by the Senones on the Adriatic coast in the area of the *ager gallicus*. Celtic mercenary activity increased particularly following the death of Alexander the Great in 323 BC and the subsequent break up of the Macedonian Empire. There was intense coming and going via Italy, with warriors seeking fame and fortune in the armies of the rivals for hegemony in the Mediterranean, and returning with new tastes and ideas from contact with the Greeks, Etruscans and the wider Mediterranean world. The conquest and settlement of northern Italy by the Celts brought them into direct contact with the Greek and Etruscan cities in the peninsula for the first time. Links with transalpine Europe were strengthened, encouraging an increased level not only of trade but also of ideas, in particular the assimilation and adaptation of new styles that had a major impact on the development of Celtic art. La Tène art is one of the most important characteristics in the definition of Celtic culture. Many of its principal elements were inspired by Etruscan or Italic models, which were in turn influenced by styles and motifs from the eastern Mediterranean. The new styles were rapidly adopted by the warrior elite. Returning from campaigns in Italy and elsewhere, they brought back

OPPOSITE A characteristic La Tène iron sword and scabbard from Gaul, 1st century BC. (Musée des Antiquités nationales, St Germain-en-Laye, France / Lauros / Giraudon / The Bridgeman Art Library)

BELOW Finely worked goblets for the consumption of highly valued Italian wine. Vessels such as these were based on Etruscan originals but were soon being adapted by Celtic craftsmen to incorporate Celtic symbols and motifs, which gave rise to the characteristic La Tène art style. (© Trustees of the British Museum / PS119291)

Detail of an Etruscan temple frieze showing a battle scene against the Celts. (akg-images / Erich Lessing)

objects made in Italo-Celtic workshops, which were then copied and adapted by Celtic artists and metalworkers with such skill and finesse that it was soon difficult to distinguish them from the originals.

The process of cultural assimilation seems to have been interrupted after the final defeat of the Senones by the Romans in 283 BC. Ever since the sack of Rome over a hundred years before, the destruction of the Senones had been a constant aim of the Romans, desperate to wipe out the shame of their defeat at the hands of the barbarians. Their first victory was gained some 40 years after they had paid off Brennus and his army of occupation, in 345 BC. Decades of constant warfare were ended by a treaty between Rome and the Senones signed in 332 BC, which brought a period of peace lasting almost 30 years. The steady growth of Roman power led to a defensive alliance between the Senones, the Etruscans and other Italic peoples. Despite their superiority in numbers, they were defeated at the battle of Sentinum in Umbria in 295 BC. In 284 BC, the Senones ambushed two legions at Arettium (Arezzo), killing the Roman consul in command. It was their last victory. The following year, Rome had its revenge: the Senones were crushed and a Roman military colony founded Sena Gallica (Senigallia) to deter rebellion. The Boii, who tried to come to their aid, were also soundly defeated. The harsh terms imposed on both tribes by Rome ensured a long period of peace.

THE BATTLE OF TELAMON, 225 BC

In the 50 years that followed the defeat of the Senones and Boii, Rome went on to conquer central and southern Italy, and captured Sicily, Corsica and Sardinia from Carthage in the First Punic War (264–241 BC). From being a small city state among many others in Italy, Rome had now established itself as one of the major powers in the Mediterranean.

Under increasing pressure from Rome, the Boii and the Insubres formed an alliance. Attempts to persuade the Cenomani to join them came to nothing; Roman bribes ensured that they and the Veneti would remain neutral. The Celts then sent envoys across the Alps to recruit mercenaries who, according to Polybius, were known as *Gaesatae*. The word can be translated as 'spearmen' or 'warriors' from the Celtic term for spear, *gaesum*. Thousands crossed into Gallia Cisalpina. At the battle of Telamon Polybius gives the strength of the Celts as 50,000 infantry and 20,000 cavalry, including a substantial number of chariots. After detaching a force to secure their flank against possible intervention by the Cenomani and Veneti, they crossed into Roman territory under the joint leadership of the chieftains Aneroestes and Concolitanus. In Rome, the population was filled with dread at the thought of the barbarian Celtic hordes once again marching on the city.

The invasion started well. The Celts defeated a Roman army at Faesulae, near Florence, and proceeded to overrun Etruria, capturing an enormous quantity of plunder, prisoners and cattle. With no further opposition they advanced towards Rome itself. Only three days' march from the city, they learnt that another Roman army, over 10,000 strong, led by the consul Aemilius Paulus, was approaching rapidly from the south, barring their path. The Celts held a council of war. Aneroestes, who was possibly the leader of the Gaesatae, argued against giving battle again and favoured a withdrawal with the booty back across the Apennines. His advice was taken and the Celts broke camp during the night and began to retreat north.

Unknown to the Celts, and in fact to Paulus, a further Roman force under the command of the second consul, Gaius Atilius, had been hurriedly withdrawn from Sardinia and had landed at Pisa, north of the Celtic position, effectively cutting off their line of retreat. From captured Celtic scouts, Atilius learned that the Celts were now caught between two Roman armies. He deployed his army and advanced to take up a favourable position near the town of Telamon on the coast, halfway between Rome and Pisa, his cavalry occupying a hill that dominated the Celts' line of retreat.

Aneroestes and Concolitanus initially supposed that Paulus' cavalry had outflanked them. A detachment of Celtic cavalry and light troops was sent forward to capture the hill. From Roman prisoners they learnt of the presence of Atilius. Faced with the enemy to the front and the rear, the Celts deployed their infantry facing both ways. The Gaesatae were placed facing Paulus with the Insubres in support. The Taurisci and the Boii faced Atilius. The cavalry and chariots were deployed on either wing while the baggage was sent to a smaller hilltop nearby under guard. Meanwhile, Paulus had learnt of Atilius' arrival and had sent his own cavalry around the flank of the Celts to reinforce the high ground.

Polybius' account of the battle of Telamon describes some of the principal characteristics displayed by a Celtic army during a major engagement at this period:

> Aemilius sending forward his cavalry to help those who were fighting on the hill … advanced to the attack. The Celtic order of battle which faced both ways was not only awe-inspiring to see but was also well suited to the needs of the situation. Facing the rear, from where they expected Aemilius to attack, the Celts had deployed the Gaesatae from beyond the Alps, and behind them the Insubres. Facing in the opposite direction, ready to meet the attack of Gaius' legions, they placed the Boii and the Taurisci. They placed their wagons and chariots at the extremity of either wing, and collected their booty on a hill with a protecting force around it. The Insubres and the Boii wore their breeches and light cloaks but the Gaesatae had discarded theirs owing to their proud confidence in themselves, and stood naked with nothing but their arms in front of the whole army.
>
> At first the battle was confined to the hill. Both sides stood watching the huge numbers of cavalry in mêlée. In this action the Consul Gaius fell, fighting desperately. The Celts took his head and brought it to their kings. However, the Roman cavalry managed at last to overcome the enemy and gained possession of the hill. The infantry now advanced towards each other. The Romans were encouraged by having caught the enemy between their two armies, but were terrified by the fine order of the Celtic host and the dreadful din, for there were numerous trumpeters and horn blowers, and the whole army was shouting its war cries at the same time. There was such a confusion of sound that it seemed to come not only from the trumpeters and warriors but also from the ground itself. No less terrifying were the appearance and gestures of the naked warriors in front, all of whom were finely built men in the prime of life, and all in the leading companies richly adorned with gold torcs and armlets. The sight of them dismayed the Romans, but the prospect of winning such spoils made them twice as keen for the fight.

When the light troops advanced in front of the legions and began to hurl their weapons in well-ordered volleys, the naked warriors in the front ranks found themselves in a difficult situation. The shield used by the Gauls does not cover the whole body, and the stature of these naked warriors made the javelins all the more likely to find their mark. After a while, unable to drive off the light troops owing to the distance and hail of javelins, their nerve broke under the ordeal. Some rushed forward in a blind fury, throwing away their lives as they tried to close with the enemy; others gave ground and fell back, creating disorder among their comrades. In this way, the martial ardour of the Gaesatae was broken.

The main body of the Insubres, Boii and Taurisci maintained a stubborn hand-to-hand combat with the Roman maniples. They held their ground, equal to their foes in courage and inferior only, as a body and as individuals, in their arms. The Roman shields were far more

Flagon fitting
made of bronze
from Brno-Maloměřice,
Moravia, 3rd century BC.
(akg-images /
Erich Lessing)

47

serviceable for defence and their swords for attack, the Celtic sword being only good for a cut and not for a thrust. Finally, attacked from higher ground and on the flank by the Roman cavalry which charged down the hill, the Celtic infantry were cut to pieces where they stood, their cavalry taking flight. About 40,000 Celts were killed and at least 10,000 taken prisoner, among them their king Concolitanus. Their other king, Aneroestes, managed to escape but was pursued and surrounded. Rather than surrender, he took his own life, along with many of his companions.

The victory encouraged the Romans to hope that they could clear the Celts from the entire valley of the Po. (*The Histories*)

Paulus took command of both Roman armies and pursued the remnants of the Celtic forces into the Po valley itself, the first Roman commander to do so. The territory of the Boii was pillaged to such an extent that the remnants of the tribe moved back to Bohemia from where they had come two centuries earlier. Within five years, the Romans had subdued all the Celtic tribes of Cisalpine Gaul. Colonies of legionary veterans were established where their presence served to intimidate the vanquished Celts and to insure against future rebellion.

'THE GREAT EXPEDITION' – THE CELTIC INVASION OF THE BALKANS

As with many legends, the story of how Segovesus, one of the nephews of the Biturigan king Ambigatus, was assigned lands in Bohemia in accordance with the wishes of the gods, may well contain a kernel of truth. The migration of Celtic-speaking peoples from central Europe eastwards along the Danube valley and into the Balkans began as early as the late 5th century BC. The apparent objective was to gain control of the amber route between the Baltic and the Mediterranean at its most strategic point, the Danube crossing west of Bratislava. A further, more widespread movement occurred in the 4th century BC, indicated by the discovery of La Tène-style objects in Slovakia, Hungary and Serbia, around Krakow in southern Poland and in many parts of the Carpathian basin. A scattering of Celtic weapons and other artefacts have even been found as far east as Moldova and Ukraine. Although most come from the graves of Scythian steppe nomads who may have obtained them through the process of gift exchange, the presence of Celtic warrior bands cannot be ruled out and may perhaps be explained by the attraction of the Greek cities on the Black Sea coast as a source of plunder or employment. Celtic shields and weapons

Magnificent iron helmet from Çiumesti, Romania, dated to the 4th century BC. The raven crest has articulated wings. (The Art Archive / National Museum Bucharest / Dagli Orti)

appear on coins from the Hellenistic kingdom of Bosporos, on the sea of Azov, and an inscription from the Greek colony of Olbia (Nikolaev, Ukraine), dating from the 3rd century BC, records that the threat of attack by the Galatoi was sufficiently serious to warrant the building of a wall to defend the city.

As with Italy, the Celtic migration into south-east Europe is confirmed by both classical sources and archaeology. Again, it is unclear what prompted this movement. The successful settlement in northern Italy, and the consequent first-hand knowledge gained by Celtic mercenaries of the wealth and weaknesses of the Mediterranean world, probably provided an impetus to other transalpine communities. Unlike the invasion of Italy, however, the attraction of rich plunder seems to have played as great a role in the Celtic incursions into Greece and the Balkans as the search for new lands to settle. By the end of the 4th century BC, the whole middle Danube region was dominated by Celtic speakers, although it remained ethnically very mixed. Archaeology suggests that the Celtic invasion of the Balkans originated from this area, which remained densely populated before and after the great expedition. Artefacts that can be linked with the Celtic migrations along the lower Danube valley and into the Balkans can be identified with La Tène styles from central Europe, in particular Bavaria and Bohemia, styles which were becoming progressively more distinct from those of the Italian and western Celts. However, there is almost no archaeological trace of the invasion of Greece, which would be virtually unknown to us were it not for the accounts of ancient Greek authors. The Greek geographer Strabo tells us that, in 335 BC, Celtic emissaries met the young Alexander of Macedon on the lower Danube while the latter was campaigning against the Thracians. Strabo believed that they had come from the Adriatic. It is quite possible that they were Senones offering their services as mercenaries. At this time in Italy a long period of almost constant warfare between the Senones and Rome was coming to an end. It is not difficult to imagine the desire of these Celtic warriors to seek employment elsewhere. In 323 BC, the Roman historian Arrian recorded that another delegation of Celts travelled all the way to Babylon, where they were received by Alexander the Great shortly before his death. The purpose of this visit which required such a long journey is not known.

Large-scale migration of groups of Celts into the Balkan peninsula only began after the death of Alexander, when the struggle for power between his generals fatally weakened the Macedonian hold on the Hellenistic world. A first expedition into Macedonia in 298 BC was repulsed. Almost 20 years later, in 281 BC, the Celts again invaded Macedonia. The army of the Macedonian king, Ptolemy Ceraunos, was crushed and Ptolemy himself killed and beheaded. Another Celtic force invaded Thrace in the same year and sacked the city of Seuthopolis. The Greek geographer Pausanias described how:

> It was then that Brennus, both in public and in private discussion with individual Galatian nobles, strongly urged a campaign against Greece, emphasizing the weakness of the country at that time, the wealth of the Greek states, and the even greater riches in the sanctuaries. In this way he persuaded the Galatians to march against Greece. Their forces amounted to over 150,000 foot and 20,000 horse. (*Description of Greece*)

Even allowing for exaggeration, the invaders came in huge numbers. This great Celtic horde, a loose confederation of peoples from many different tribes, began to move south into Macedonia in 280 BC. Only three years before, the Romans had broken the power of the Senones in Italy. It is not unlikely that some, perhaps many, Italian Celts decided to throw in their lot with Brennus. In 279 BC, the invasion of Greece began in earnest. Quarrelling among the leaders of the various factions caused a split even before the Celts entered Greece. A substantial portion, perhaps as much as one-third, led by Leonorios and Lutorios, decided to move towards Thrace while the majority, under Brennus and Acichorios, continued south heading for the great sanctuary of Apollo at Delphi, the holiest site in Greece, leaving behind them a small force to secure Macedonia.

At first, the Celts met little opposition. Their alleged savage reputation preceded them: tales of wholesale butchery and cannibalism, with even their own dead being left without burial – the ultimate barbarity in the eyes of the Greeks who believed that if the body were not buried the soul would be left to wander the earth. All who could sought the shelter and protection of the cities, which the Celts, lacking any kind of siege equipment, were unable to attack. A Greek army led by Athens took up a position to defend the pass of Thermopylae, as Leonidas' Spartans had done against the Persians under Darius in 480 BC. At first the Greeks beat them back, inflicting heavy losses. However, just as Darius' forces had done 200 years previously, so too did the Celts find a path through the mountains that enabled them to outflank the defenders. The Celtic host now split up even further. Acichorios marched west into Aetolia where his force sacked the city of Callium; Brennus headed directly for Delphi. It was now almost the middle of winter. The Greeks massed against them, calling on the gods for help. Pausanias described how Apollo came to their aid:

> Brennus and his army were now faced by the Greeks who had gathered at Delphi. Soon, portents which boded no good for the barbarians were sent by the god. The whole ground occupied by the Galatian army was shaken violently, with continuous thunder and lightning. The thunder terrified the Galatians and prevented them from hearing their orders, while the bolts from heaven set on fire not only those whom they struck but also their neighbours.
> (*Description of Greece*)

The site of Apollo's shrine at Delphi lies at the intersection of two geological fault lines and is one of the places in Europe most prone to earthquakes. The trance that the priestess of Apollo, known as the Pythoness, experienced when in communion with the god is thought to be caused in part by the fumes escaping from deep below the surface. If there was indeed an earthquake at this precise moment, then the Greeks surely felt justified in claiming that divine intervention helped them overcome

The temple of
Apollo at Delphi.
(C. Hellier / Ancient
Art & Architecture
Collection Ltd)

the invaders. The Greek claim that the sanctuary at Delphi was saved from the depredations of the barbarians is disputed by other ancient authors, who believed that it had been plundered by the Celts before they were defeated. Brennus is said to have mocked the statues of the Greek gods, and it was alleged much later that part of the treasure looted by the Romans from the Celtic shrine in Tolosa (Toulouse) in south-west France had originally come from Delphi. In any event, at dawn the following day, the Celts faced the Greek army elated by the knowledge that the gods were with them. Now, it was the turn of the Celts to be attacked from the front and in the flank. Despite serious losses, they resisted strongly until Brennus fell wounded. They retreated stubbornly, killing their wounded rather than leaving them to the mercy of the Greeks. The earth is said to have trembled again that night. Celtic losses amounted to over 25,000 dead. In desperation, Brennus took his own life.

The great expedition had failed. Acichorios led the survivors in a disorderly retreat, harassed by the Greeks. The Celtic host fell apart. Many returned to settle in the Danube valley near the confluence of the Danube and Sava rivers, where they were later known as the Scordisci. Their main centre became Singidunum, the modern Belgrade. The Scordisci remained a powerful Celtic group for over two centuries, continuing to raid Macedonia and Greece, and successfully repelling the Cimbri and Teutones, a mix of Celtic and Germanic tribes who migrated south from the Jutland peninsula at the end of the 2nd century BC. Others returned to Macedonia only to be defeated in 277 BC by the new king, Antigonos Gonatos, who recruited many into his own army. Antigonos' rival, Pyrrhus of Epirus, apparently boasted of the number of Celtic mercenaries he had killed. The site of the defeat by Antigonos was somewhere near the Gallipoli peninsula, which suggests that these Celts were attempting to follow the route taken by Lutorios and Leonorios. A smaller group eventually reached the Black Sea coast and founded the kingdom of Tylis, from where they terrorized neighbouring Greek colonies until they were conquered by the Thracians at the end of the 3rd century BC. Their presence has left little trace in the archaeological record, although at Mezek in Bulgaria, not far from the Turkish border, an elite chariot burial with La Tène artefacts has been discovered, dating from the first half of the 3rd century BC. It is unclear, however, whether this was a Celtic or a Thracian burial. A better indication of assimilation between Celts and Thracians is the famous Gundestrup cauldron (see pp.58–59), named after the site in Denmark where it was discovered. This magnificent example of Celtic art is decorated with images of Celtic gods and warriors, but includes many elements that are clearly Thracian and also oriental in origin.

THE GALATIANS IN ASIA MINOR

The Celts led by Lutorios and Leonorios who did not join Brennus and Acichorios on their ill-fated invasion of Greece crossed the Hellespont into Asia Minor in 278 BC at the invitation of Nicomedes, king of Bithynia. Perhaps their aim had always been to find new land to settle, whereas Brennus had been more interested in loot. They were made up of three tribes: the Tectosages, the Trocmii and the Tolistobogii. Nicomedes intended to employ his Galatian mercenaries against the Seleucid king of Syria, Antiochus I, who ruled most of what is now modern Turkey. Antiochus defeated them in 275 BC although subsequently, in alliance with Mithridates, king of Pontus, they settled on the plateau region along the river Halys, land which belonged to the Seleucids and from where Antiochus II was unable to dislodge them. The land on which they settled became known as Galatia. Archaeology has so far revealed few Celtic remains in Asia Minor; excavations suggest that the material culture of the Galatians quickly became Hellenized. Yet they seem to have resisted assimilation for a considerable period, retaining their Celtic language for centuries. In the 4th century AD, St Jerome wrote that the language of the Galatians was similar to that spoken by the Gauls. From their new homeland, they raided the rich surrounding states, earning themselves a grim reputation for savagery and slave trading. Hellenistic rulers made use of this reputation by hiring them as mercenaries and incorporating large numbers into their armies. They fought among themselves and terrorized their neighbours, as well as continuing to supply mercenaries to whoever would pay. Each tribe had an agreed area to raid. The area around the Dardanelles was the preserve of the Trocmii, the Tolistobogii raided the rich Greek cities of the Ionian coast, while the Tectosages concentrated their efforts inland. Galatia soon became a great slave-trading centre. Special taxes were raised by the Greek cities to ransom prisoners taken in raids, but rumours of unransomed or unsold prisoners being sacrificed to the bloodthirsty Celtic gods made many prefer to commit suicide rather than fall into the hands of the Galatoi.

Other Celtic bands were recruited as mercenaries into the army of Ptolemy Philadelphos, the Greek ruler of Egypt. He soon discovered that they were a mixed blessing. Their attempt at rebellion was discovered, and 4,000 were confined on an island in the Nile. Rather than face an ignoble death by starvation, they chose to commit suicide. Nevertheless, Celtic mercenaries continued to be hired by Egyptian rulers. When discharged, they were granted land to settle in return for duty as reservists.

Rome first came into contact with the Galatians at the battle of Magnesia in 190 BC, when they formed a contingent in the army of Antiochus III of Seleucia. The Roman victory in the battle was followed by a punitive expedition against their capital at Ancyra, which drastically reduced their capability to terrorize their neighbours. However, Rome recognized their value in the shifting political environment of the Hellenistic east and left them a degree of power under Roman hegemony. A century later, this hegemony was challenged by Mithridates of Pontus, whose ambition was to expel the Romans from Asia Minor and even from Greece itself. He began by attacking Rome's allies. In an attempt to nullify the threat from the Galatians, he had their leaders and their families massacred at Pergamon, having lured them there with false assurances of his peaceful intentions. His actions ensured that the Galatians would fight alongside the Romans commanded by Pompey, Caesar's future rival. Mithridates was defeated in 66 BC. The Galatians became a Roman client state under the patronage of Pompey, who established a single ruler for each of the three tribes. Deiotarus of the Tolistobogii emerged as the pre-eminent leader and was regarded as sole king by the Romans. He supported Pompey in the civil war against Caesar, but also survived the defeat and assassination of his patron. His grandson, Amyntas, was the last independent ruler of the Galatians. On his death in 25 BC, Galatia was incorporated as a province into the Roman Empire.

MIGRATIONS TO THE WEST

For the Celts themselves, one of the principal consequences of their migrations to south-east Europe and their incursions into the Balkans and Greece was the loosening of traditional social ties and the formation of new tribal groups that were often ethnically very mixed. The defeat and collapse of the Celtic armies under Brennus and Acichorios intensified this process. Those who survived the retreat from Delphi and returned to the Danube valley had no identity beyond that of the group among whom they had lived and fought during the campaign. Many had no desire to go back to old ways of living; others knew no other life except as part of a wandering band. Despite the failure of the great expedition, they would continue to live by the sword. As such, they began to look for new opportunities for employment. Some accepted service in the army of their former opponent, Antigonos Gonatos, king of Macedon. Others looked to the west.

The discovery of objects in the distinctive Danubian La Tène style clearly shows that bands of Celtic warriors and their families migrated in substantial numbers from the middle Danube region to several areas of western Europe about the middle of the 3rd century BC. The Volcae Tectosages eventually settled in the valley of the Garonne, in south-west France near the Pyrenees, between 275 and 260 BC. Perhaps they were related to the Tectosages who settled in Asia Minor, or perhaps they merely shared a similar name, interpreted as 'the Wolves with no Home' – literally, 'with no roof'. Why they should have chosen to settle there is not known. Their future tribal centre, Tolosa (the modern city of Toulouse), would dominate the ancient trade route between the Mediterranean and the Atlantic. Another explanation could be the proximity of Carthaginian territory over the mountains in Iberia with its opportunities for further mercenary recruitment.

The migration of new Celtic groups to the Rhône valley is also indicated by the appearance of Danubian artefacts. Polybius wrote about the Gaesatae, who were recruited as mercenaries by the Insubres and Boii of Cisalpine Gaul to aid them against the growing threat of Rome. He was probably referring to the Allobroges, whose name is thought to signify 'those who come from elsewhere'. The Carthaginian general Hannibal found them living between the Rhône and

Silver tetradrachma of Philip II of Macedon, 4th century BC. The use of coinage was introduced into the Celtic world via Italy in part by returning mercenaries who had been paid with coins such as these. (Schweizerisches Landesmuseum, Zürich, DIA-8523, 8524)

Circular bronze harness plaque discovered in a chariot grave at Somme-Brionne, France. It is considered to be one of the finest surviving artefacts of the early La Tène period, early 5th century BC. (Werner Forman Archive / British Museum, London)

the Isère when marching from Iberia to invade Italy at the start of the Second Punic War in 218 BC. Many of them and many Cisalpine Gauls may have joined forces with him to avenge the defeat of Telamon. Polybius records that Hannibal's army included large numbers of Celtic mercenaries, though at the battle of the Trebbia Celts fought on both sides. Hannibal's mercenaries played a leading role in his greatest victory against Rome at Cannae in 216 BC.

Further north, in the Champagne region, other groups began to reoccupy the areas depopulated by the departure of the Senones in the 5th century BC from around 270 BC. Female jewellery in the typical Danubian style distinguishes these groups from the indigenous Celtic inhabitants. Although they adopted some local customs, they retained the usual La Tène male burial rituals with sword, spear and shield. These groups can probably be identified with the Belgae, whom Caesar considered different from the Celts living south of the rivers Seine and Marne, and whom he described as the most warlike of the Gauls. The aggression of these military groups continued to lead to conflicts after they had settled permanently. The turbulent evolution of the new tribes in northern Gaul is reflected by monuments and sanctuaries such as those at Gournay-sur-Aronde and Ribemont-sur-Ancre, where quantities of weapons and spoils of the dead testify to the violence that persisted in the region.

THE NATURE OF THE CELTIC MIGRATIONS

According to the Greek author Strabo, quoted at the beginning of this chapter, the Celts were always ready to seek out new land and to move with family and possessions almost at a whim. However, this view is based mainly on Caesar's description of the migration of the Helvetii, and takes no account of the different social and political circumstances that existed elsewhere and at other times. The migration of the Helvetii concerned the mass movement of a people already uprooted by Germanic pressure, in a Celtic world under threat. The situation was very different in the 4th and 3rd centuries BC, when the Celtic world was at the peak of its strength and no tribe was obliged to leave its ancestral territory. Archaeological evidence supports this. Wherever evidence indicates a possible point of origin for the Celtic migrations, it is always in a densely populated region. There is no discernable break, although the departure of large groups could entail a fall in the overall level of population, as for example in the Marnian zone after the beginning of the 4th century BC. It is perhaps more appropriate to consider the expansion of Celtic-speaking peoples in the 4th and 3rd centuries BC as a form of colonization caused mainly by a surplus population rather than a migration in the true sense of the word. It can be likened to the Greek colonization of the Mediterranean and Black Sea coasts in the 7th and 6th centuries BC and the Viking expansion at the end of the 1st millennium AD rather than to the Germanic migrations that contributed to the collapse of the western Roman Empire in the 5th century AD.

The migrations to south-eastern Europe and Asia Minor mark the furthest extent of the Celtic world. The destruction of the Senones, probably the most powerful Celtic tribe in Italy, and the defeat of Brennus' army at Delphi at almost the same time, marked a turning point. Thereafter, the Celts would come under increasing pressure, not only from the Romans but also from threats elsewhere. Their domination of much of central and western Europe would slowly diminish over the last two centuries BC. They did not give it up without a struggle.

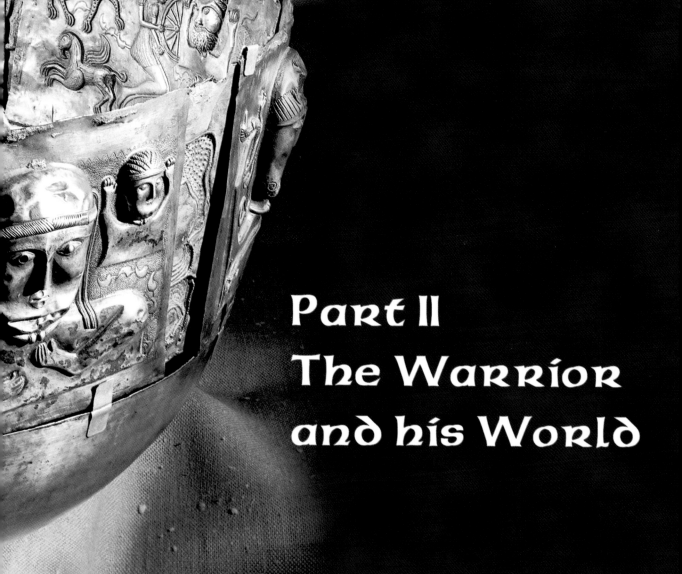

Part II
The Warrior
and his World

CHAPTER 3

THE BONDS OF SOCIETY

In Gaul there are only two classes of men who are of any account or consideration. The common people are little better than slaves … The two privileged classes are the Druids and the nobility. (Caesar, The Conquest of Gaul)

A SOCIETY IN TRANSITION

Ancient Celtic society has often been described as 'heroic', in the sense that it was dominated by a warrior elite whose lives were spent in an environment of perpetual conflict. Rich grave goods, including weapons and armour, together with later myths and legends, have reinforced this image. Archaeologists point out, however, that such finds will only be relevant to the social elite and that the overwhelming majority of the population of Iron Age Europe was far more concerned with the plough than with the sword. Nevertheless, taken as a whole, the evidence we possess reveals a world in which warfare and conflict were endemic and played an essential part in maintaining the structure of Celtic society itself.

Celtic society experienced enormous changes between the 6th and 1st centuries BC. Unfortunately, as mentioned previously, it is difficult to form a coherent picture because the evidence that is available to us is unevenly distributed, both geographically and chronologically. Classical authors provide a great deal of useful information, albeit from their own perspectives, concerning the Celts who settled in northern Italy in the 4th century BC and those who took part in the invasion of the Balkans in the 3rd century BC. The society of the Galatians who settled in Asia Minor is well documented by Greek writers, while Caesar provides an extensive account of late Gallic society in the 1st century BC in his *Commentaries on the Gallic War*. The only picture we have of a Celtic society that is not described by classical sources comes from pre-Christian Ireland, the only part of the Celtic-speaking world to remain free of the domination of

This assembly of grave goods, dated to the 1st century BC, includes wine amphorae and other items intended for use at the feast in the Otherworld. (akg-images / Erich Lessing)

Rome. Unlike the Celts in continental Europe, the Irish were able to preserve both their language and their oral traditions, which provide a tantalizing glimpse of what the oral literature of other Celtic peoples may have been like.

Ancient Irish myth and legend portray a society that can be compared with that of the Halstatt Celts of the early Iron Age. The richly furnished tombs of high-status men and women containing foreign prestige goods suggest that the role they played in the life of their communities was very much like that of a royal dynasty. The Halstatt Princedoms of continental Europe were brought down during the 5th century BC by the rise of groups of Celtic peoples whose social structure was dominated by a warrior aristocracy. The migrations that these warrior societies undertook over the next 200 years effectively broke the bond between the tribe and its ancestral territory. The institution of kingship declined among the continental Celts throughout the Migration Period as tribes split up and coalesced into new communities. During this time, the Celts are often described as being led by two leaders: Aneroestes and Concolitanus at the battle of Telamon, Brennus and Acichorios in the great raid on the sanctuary at Delphi, and Leonorios and Lutorios who led the Galatians into Asia Minor, an interesting contemporary parallel with the system of government of the Roman Republic, in which two consuls were elected annually to preside over the Senate. By the 1st century BC, Celtic kings ruled only in Britain and Ireland. Gaul was dominated by powerful tribal confederations called *civitates* by the Romans, ruled by an oligarchy of great aristocratic families.

Drinking horn decorated with bronze and gold from the tomb of the Hochdorf Prince. (Landesmuseum Württemberg Stuttgart; P. Frankenstein, H. Zwietasch)

HIGH KINGS AND HEROES – THE STRUCTURE OF EARLY CELTIC SOCIETY

Early Celtic society was organized by descent through the male line from a common ancestor, real or mythical, with the head of the household representing the incarnation of the guardian divinity of the family. At its lowest level, Celtic society was made up of extended families or clans that were grouped together to form territorially based tribes. In ancient Ireland, the basic family unit, the *fine*, encompassed several generations. Five families, with a common ancestor, made up a clan. Several clans that shared the same territory formed a *tuath*, or tribe, ruled by a king. Large settlements were rare except for the fortified enclosures of these petty kings and the 'royal' sites, such as Tara. The landscape was dotted with farmsteads and small hamlets. Land could not be privately owned, but was held in common by the clan. As with almost all ancient societies, agriculture formed the economic basis of the Celtic world. By the beginning of the La Tène period, Celtic agriculture had developed to a level where it was able to produce surpluses beyond the everyday needs of the population. Celtic society was therefore able to support an aristocratic elite and a specialist class of craftsmen, and to develop the sophisticated trading system that eventually led to the beginnings of an urban civilization, especially in Gaul. Experimental archaeology has demonstrated that varieties of ancient wheat such as emmer, spelt and einkorn could produce harvests larger than those usually achieved in the Middle Ages. Perhaps surprisingly, they have even been found to produce harvests that are often larger than those achieved under similar conditions from modern varieties (which are also poorer in protein and have lower nutritional value). Barley was also cultivated, from which the Celts made a form of beer that they called *cervesia*. The name is still preserved today in the French *cervoise* and the Spanish *cerveza*.

Livestock played an essential role in Celtic society. One of the greatest tales in Irish mythology, the *Táin Bó Cúailnge* ('The Cattle Raid of Cooley'), concerns the war between the kingdoms of Ulster and Connaught that was fought as the result of the theft of the divine brown bull of Cooley. The status of Celtic nobles depended more on the number of cattle they owned than on the amount of land that was cultivated on their behalf by their tenants. Cattle and pork accounted for most of the meat they consumed. Celtic ham and other similar products were famous and exported as far as Italy. The ability to preserve food, which became widespread with the increase in salt mining around the beginning of the 1st millennium BC, greatly facilitated the mobility of later Celtic populations. Hunting was mainly a pastime reserved for the nobility and does not seem to have contributed very much to the diet of the ordinary people.

The Great Roundhouse, Butser Ancient Farm in Hampshire. A modern reconstruction of the characteristic British Iron Age dwellings, which differed from their rectangular continental equivalents. (Author's collection)

Silvered iron torc with bull heads, 2nd century BC. (akg-images / Erich Lessing)

According to the image of ancient Irish society presented in myth and legend, the social hierarchy was defined by the possession of cattle. Polybius wrote in *The Histories* of the Celts of northern Italy, 'Their possessions consist of cattle and gold because these are the only things they can carry around with them everywhere according to circumstance.' Those who owned livestock were accounted free in the eyes of the law. They had the right to bear arms and participate in the tribal assembly that elected the king and in theory approve, or at least endorse, all major decisions, such as declarations of war. However, real power was wielded by the noble elite, the warrior aristocracy that Caesar referred to as a 'senate'.

Classical texts tell us little about the common people who made up the vast majority of the population of Celtic communities. While they were not all slaves in the sense of the Mediterranean world, many were 'unfree', without legal status. The Druids, mentioned by Caesar as being one of the two principal classes in Gallic society, formed part of the privileged class known in Ireland as 'men of art', which also included bards, who extolled the virtues of the warrior hero in poetry and song. Craftsmen, especially blacksmiths and other metalworkers who manufactured not only everyday tools, but also the weapons, jewellery and other finery worn by the

Celtic nobles to emphasize their wealth and rank, were also considered to be men of art and enjoyed high status in Celtic society. The remarkable skill of Celtic craftsmen created the La Tène artistic style that defined later Celtic culture by the adaptation of Etruscan and other Mediterranean forms to existing native styles. Their skill is most apparent in weaponry and jewellery. Blacksmiths made the warriors' weapons – high-quality spears and swords – by mixing different grades of iron; jewellery and ornamentation were the speciality of those who worked with gold, silver and bronze. Coral, the only raw material imported into transalpine Europe from the Mediterranean and regarded by the Celts as possessing particular otherworldly power, was used as an inlay and appliqué on metal. When the technique of direct fusion onto an object was perfected in the 3rd century BC, red glass and enamel became the preferred materials for the embellishment of both arms and jewellery. The skill of Celtic metalworkers was known and envied throughout the classical world. Masters of their art and of the symbolic language of the gods, these Celtic craftsmen produced objects of subtle designs and decoration that were imbued with the power of the supernatural.

CLIENTAGE AND FOSTERING

Celtic society was bound together by a complex web of family ties and mutual dependence. The basis for this was the custom of clientage that established a bond of mutual obligation between individuals of different status, in particular allegiance in war. Originally the bond concerned the higher-status patron placing his livestock into the safekeeping of the lower-status client. According to ancient Irish tradition, such bonds were normally of three years' duration, the length of time between major tribal assemblies at which vows of allegiance and other contracts were renewed. It was an agreement closely bound up with personal honour, and there were dire consequences for any who did not respect their obligations. In return for protection and patronage, the client would agree to surrender his legal rights in favour of his patron. These were determined by his 'honour price', the equivalent of the Anglo-Saxon custom of *wergild*, the amount payable by a third party in the event of unlawful injury or death. The concept of honour price was fundamental to the legal system of the Celts. It dictated the conduct of all judicial cases, since the value of an individual's oath or evidence was determined by his honour price. To bring a lawsuit against someone with a higher honour price required the intervention of a patron of higher rank, creating an environment in which the support of the richest and most influential members of the elite was constantly sought after. Equally intense was the rivalry among the nobility to acquire the greatest number of clients. A large retinue was a reflection of the noble's standing in Celtic social hierarchy: 'They treated comradeship as of the greatest importance, those among them being the most feared and most powerful who were thought to have the largest number of attendants and associates.' (Polybius, *The Histories*)

Clientage could also extend to other tribes and even among tribes themselves. For example, the rival Aedui and Sequani each had their respective client tribes in Gaul at the time of Caesar's campaigns. The system was reinforced by the fostering of children into the household of a patron until they reached adulthood, 14 for girls and 17 for boys. The legend of King Arthur tells how the young prince Arthur was brought up in secret in the household of Sir Ector together with his foster brother Cai. In the *Táin*, the newborn hero Cúchulainn is given into the care of his aunt, the sister of his father the king, and also of the king's closest retainers. The following comment by Caesar can be interpreted as a reference to the continued existence of the custom at the time of the Gallic War in the mid-1st century BC: 'They do not permit their sons to approach them openly until they are of an age to bear arms, and they regard it as indecorous for a young son to stand in public in the presence of his father.' (*The Conquest of Gaul*)

Children of freemen were sent to the households of richer patrons; the aristocracy sent their offspring to the families of the most powerful nobles, and often

Replica 'Crannog', Graggaunowen, County Clare, Ireland, consisting of a group of palisaded buildings on an artificial island or platform raised on stilts over water. This type of settlement was common in parts of Ireland and Scotland from the Bronze Age to the mediaeval period. (Werner Forman Archive)

to royal families. Sons and daughters of kings went to other royal families. Fostering ensured not only an upbringing in a higher social environment, but also a certain level of security by the presence of potential hostages. Perhaps most important of all, it established bonds of loyalty that were often stronger than ties of blood:

Reconstruction of a Gallic farm, L'Archéodrome, Beaune. (Author's collection)

> Whenever war breaks out and their services are required, they all take the field surrounded by their retainers and dependants of whom each noble has a greater or smaller number according to his birth and fortune. The possession of such a following is the only criterion of influence and power that they recognize. (Caesar, *The Conquest of Gaul*)

FEASTING, STATUS AND WAR

In ancient Irish tradition, the king was responsible for maintaining the sacred harmony between the tribe and the land, and thus ensuring the continued prosperity of the community. The legendary Conn represented the ideal model of Celtic kingship. In his reign it was said that the earth was worked only a fortnight a month in springtime and gave three harvests a year.

The essential qualities required in a king in order to ensure harmony and prosperity were strength to defend the land over which he ruled, and generosity towards those who had chosen him to personify the community and who would follow him in peace and war. A king who could not lead them to victory on the battlefield or who was physically impaired in some way would be replaced or even eliminated; one who did not share his wealth was considered to oppose the natural order of things, which would also lead to the king's speedy removal from the throne. It was therefore the king's responsibility to provide gifts, often foreign luxury goods, for the elite of the tribe: the nobility, the warrior heroes, Druids, poets and craftsmen. The value of such gifts was measured by the influence they could command in being given away. This method of redistributing prestige items to increase influence and status is known as *potlach*.

The majority of the foreign luxury goods imported into transalpine Europe from the Mediterranean involved the consumption of wine. Wine's popularity and rapid

adoption into traditional Celtic social customs partly explains the incredulity of the Greek historian Diodorus Siculus when he wrote, 'The Gauls are exceedingly addicted to wine brought into their country by merchants who receive an incredible price for it: a slave in exchange for a jar of wine.' (*Historical Library*) The Roman merchant doubtless believed that he was getting the best of the bargain, but the Celts knew the value of the deal. Slaves were easy to obtain, while sharing the wine freely would reinforce the king's or the noble's standing in the tribe as a man of substance and largesse whom others would wish to follow and share in his wealth. Another Greek writer, Poseidonius, who visited southern Gaul in the early 1st century BC, provides a fascinating first-hand account of some of the social customs of the Gauls. Although his original works have not survived, they were widely used by other classical authors. Here, he tells of a Gallic noble named Louvernius:

> In an attempt to win popular favour [he] rode across the country in a chariot distributing gold and silver to those who followed him. Moreover, he set up an enclosure one and a half miles on each side within which he filled vats with expensive liquor and prepared so great a quantity of food that for many days all who wished could come and enjoy the feast. (*Histories*, quoted by Athenaeus)

The feast was an important element in the structure of Celtic society. These social gatherings, given by the king or the noble elite, were usually wild and drunken, sometimes deadly, and often with ritual significance. They were attended by both free men and women, whose presence was obligatory. A strict ceremonial procedure was observed with regard to precedence and hospitality. Seating was arranged according to rank and was divided between the high-status guests who sat in the hall and the less prosperous and younger who remained outside, as Poseidonius writes:

> They sit in a circle with the most influential man in the centre whether he be the greatest in warlike skill, nobility of family or wealth. Beside him sits the host and on either side of them the others in order of distinction. Their shield bearers stand behind them while their spearmen are seated on the opposite side and feast in common like their lords. (*Histories*, quoted by Athenaeus)

Also in attendance at the feast were bards and poets who would demonstrate their own craft and learning. They recounted the lineage, bravery and wealth of the host and his ancestors as well as the deeds of legendary heroes. Their songs, however, could

OPPOSITE The famous Basse-Yutz flagons from Lorraine, made from bronze and decorated with coral and red enamel inlay. Dated to c. 400 BC, flagons such as these were modelled on simpler Etruscan designs. The hunting motif illustrated on the handles and spouts suggests that such objects were used by the Celtic aristocracy. (Werner Forman Archive / British Museum, London) either praise or satirize, and fear of losing face in front of the guests encouraged the host to even greater acts of generosity. Poseidonius continues the tale of Louvernius:

> A poet who arrived late met Louvernius and composed a song praising his greatness and lamenting his own late arrival. Louvernius threw a bag of gold to the bard, who ran beside his chariot and sang another song saying that the very tracks of his chariot gave gold and largesse. (*Histories*, quoted by Athenaeus)

Detail of one of the Basse-Yutz flagons showing the remarkable degree of workmanship. (Werner Forman Archive / British Museum, London)

Strangers were allowed to share the meal before being asked their name and business. Food and drink were served according to status. Traditionally, the greatest warrior received the choicest cut of pork, the champion's portion of the thigh piece. This was the moment when any other warrior had the right to dispute his position and challenge him. Drunkenness would often cause other disputes that would escalate into more serious violence. Poseidonius continues his commentary:

> The Celts sometimes engage in single combat at dinner. Assembling in arms, they engage in mock battle drill and mutual thrust and parry. Sometimes wounds are inflicted and the irritation caused by this may even lead to the killing of the opponent unless they are held back by friends. When the hindquarters are served up, the bravest takes the thigh piece; if another man claims it they stand up and fight in single combat to the death. (*Histories*, quoted by Athenaeus)

Poseidonius also describes an extreme gesture of *potlach* in the context of a feast:

> In the presence of the assembly, a warrior received silver or gold or a certain number of jars of wine, and having distributed the gifts among his friends and kin, lay stretched out face upwards on his shield. Another warrior then cut his throat with his sword. (*Histories*, quoted by Athenaeus)

We should probably view such an extraordinary act in the context of the constant competition for status among the Celtic nobility. The feasting, the consumption of wine and a belief in life after death should all be taken into account. That an individual was prepared to die in this manner would undoubtedly ensure that he would be remembered as a man of renown.

Amidst the drinking, boasting and singing, one of the warriors might propose to lead a raid and would encourage others to join him, tempting them with the prospect of loot and glory. The number of men who agreed to follow was determined by his status. The more volunteers he could recruit, the greater would be the chances of a successful outcome. A raid that brought spoils for him to distribute among his followers would further enhance his status as a leader. On a future occasion he would then be able to attract an even larger retinue, which in turn would have higher expectations of success and loot to be gained. Small-scale raids on neighbouring clans to reive a few head of cattle would grow into inter-tribal conflicts and wider raiding over greater distances. Groups of warriors fighting as mercenaries in foreign armies were a logical step in this process. Once established, this cycle of conflict fed on itself and became essential to the maintenance of early Celtic society.

Gold armbands and earrings found in the 'La Butte' grave mound in Burgundy, France, 6th century BC. (akg-images / Archives CDA / Guillo)

A WOMAN'S PLACE

The discovery and excavation of the tomb of the Vix Princess and other female graves of the Halstatt period clearly demonstrates the high status of some women in early Celtic society. From the accounts in ancient Irish myths and legends, such women apparently enjoyed the same rights as men, although these rights were dictated by the individual's place in the social hierarchy. A noblewoman could own property in her own right, choose her own husband, divorce him at will, accompany him to war and even fight alongside him. Diodorus Siculus wrote that the women of Gaul were not only like their menfolk in their great stature, but were a match for them in courage as well. This quality was depicted, probably in caricature, by the Roman author Ammianus Marcellinus in the 4th century AD:

> A whole band of foreigners will be unable to cope with one of [the Gauls] in a fight if he calls
> in his wife, stronger than he by far and with flashing eyes, least of all when she swells her neck
> and gnashes her teeth, and raising her huge white arms, she rains blows and kicks like shots
> discharged by the twisted cords of a catapult. (*The Late Roman Empire*)

The hero Cúchulainn was said to have received instruction in the arts of war from the Druidess Scarthach. A woman of royal descent could succeed to the throne in the absence of a male heir, and could rule in her own right, rather than through her husband, if she were married. Perhaps the most famous example of this is Boudica, who became queen of the Iceni on the death of her husband at the time of the Roman conquest of Britain (see pp.186–90). Another, again in Britain at the same period, is Cartimandua, queen of the Brigantes, who divorced her husband and married one of his closest retainers. The question of women wielding power in Celtic society remains unclear, however. We know of no other female rulers among the Celts apart from Boudica and Cartimandua, whose influence may be a consequence of the upheaval caused by the Roman invasion of Britain.

According to Caesar, Celtic men had one principal wife; others could be taken, but were considered of lower rank or merely as concubines. Despite his remark that a husband also had the power of life and death over his wife and children, it is clear from the following comment that marriage was far more a contract between equals among the Celts than in Roman society:

> The men take from their own goods a sum equal to the dowry that they received from their wives and place it with the dowry. An account of each sum is kept between them and the profits saved. Whichever of the two survives receives both portions together with the profits. (Caesar, *The Conquest of Gaul*)

Nevertheless, the privileged position of Celtic noblewomen was tempered by the obligations of the political and dynastic marriages with which alliances within and between tribes were usually sealed.

Gold coin minted by the Bituriges, 1st century BC. Note the classical-style head and the stylized chariot warrior common on many Celtic coins, possibly representing a god or a mythological hero. (Schweizerisches Landesmuseum, Zürich, COL-21145, 21146)

THE EVOLUTION OF CELTIC URBAN CIVILIZATION

The continual competition for wealth, power and status among the Celtic elite created a situation that was inherently unstable. This may have been one of the causes of the disruption that occurred in many parts of western and central Europe at the time of the Celtic migrations. However, from the latter half of the 3rd century BC, archaeological evidence indicates that the formation of new and powerful tribal confederations in transalpine Europe slowly restored a degree of stability to Celtic society.

Maiden Castle, in Dorset, England, is the largest hillfort in Europe. Recent research has called into question the theory that it was the site of a major battle between the British Durotriges and the Romans under the future Emperor Vespasian in AD 43. (© John Farmar; Cordaiy Photo Library Ltd / CORBIS)

One of the most significant factors in the development of Celtic society at this period was the introduction of the use of coinage. The Celts of northern Italy were already accustomed to using coins as a medium of exchange instead of barter. Returning Celtic mercenaries who had been paid in cash by their Mediterranean employers were probably responsible for introducing it into the Celtic world north of the Alps. In Bohemia, the Boii favoured the gold stater of Philip II of Macedon, which continued to be struck long after his death, becoming a sort of 'dollar of the ancient world'. The Belgae of northern Gaul preferred the stater of Tarentum, a Greek city at the southern tip of Italy that had always been a major employer of Celtic mercenaries. Within a very short time, however, Celtic gold and silversmiths were producing their own imitations of Greek and Macedonian originals. It is perhaps no coincidence that the first local coinages were produced in the Rhône valley at the same time as the settlement of the Allobroges, who may have been the Gaesatae mentioned by Polybius. Celtic metalworkers also began to interpret and rework the images on the coins to portray their own heroes and ancestors. Thus, the head on the obverse now often appeared with a torc or other symbol, while the reverse featured a chariot or horse. From the 2nd century BC onwards, different communities can be identified by the images on the local coins. The introduction of sub-divisions of coins made them more convenient to use in everyday commercial life rather than merely in large-scale transactions such as the payment of tribute.

A further stage in the evolution of Celtic society, and an indication of the economic growth and prosperity of Celtic Europe, is the appearance of a new type of settlement. Polybius referred to such a settlement as a *polis*, while Caesar used the term *oppidum*. Both terms designate an enclosed site, and also a 'town' or 'city', suggesting that they were sufficiently recognizable in the eyes of both Greeks and Romans to merit such a description. They can be traced back to the hillforts of the Halstatt Princedoms and the preceding Bronze Age, but, unlike their predecessors, they were not all situated on hilltops. While making the best use of existing natural features, they were established on important trade routes, often near river crossings or at the mouths of valleys. The modern definition of an oppidum (plural: *oppida*) is based on Caesar's account of those he encountered in Gaul: a large, often fortified urban centre, which is usually considered to be a tribal stronghold in view of its size and density of population, and because of the variety of artisan, commercial, administrative and religious activities that were carried on there. More than 200 oppida have been discovered across Europe, from southern Britain to the middle Danube, and from central Spain to northern Italy. Many survived to become the foundations of modern European cities, including Colchester, Paris, Milan, Geneva, Budapest and Salamanca. Fortunately for us, Bibracte, in modern France, one of the most important of all Celtic oppida, did not become overlaid with 2,000 years of further urban development and, as a consequence, has been the subject of extensive and continuing excavation.

In 58 BC, Caesar described Bibracte as 'by far the largest and richest oppidum of the Aedui'. The Aedui were one of the most powerful and influential Celtic tribes of central Gaul in the 1st century BC. Throughout most of Caesar's campaigns, they remained loyal to the treaty of friendship that they had signed with Rome almost three-quarters of a century before. On several occasions during his campaigns in Gaul, Caesar used Bibracte as his winter quarters and centre of operations. Bibracte was abandoned at the end of the 1st century BC when the Aedui established a new urban centre, either voluntarily or 'encouraged' by the Romans, on a new site on lower ground nearer to the river Saône. In honour of the emperor, it was named Augustodunum, the modern French town of Autun. Bibracte was located on the summit of Mont Beuvray, some 25km (15½ miles) to the west of Autun, on a hilltop site that controlled a number of important trade routes between northern and southern Gaul. Large-scale excavations since the early 1980s have revealed the extent of this remarkable Celtic city. Covering an area of 135 hectares (334 acres), it was surrounded by a rampart over 5km (3 miles) long. Its permanent

Silver coin from Gaul with the name Dumnorix, one of the leaders of the Aedui, 1st century BC. (akg-images / Erich Lessing)

Reconstruction
of the murus gallicus
at the entrance to the
oppidum of Bibracte.
(Author's collection)

population is believed to have been at least several thousand. The traces of many wooden and stone structures have been found, some with a floor area of 100m² (1,076ft²) and often with a second level, indicating the existence of an elaborate street plan and of different zones devoted to a variety of commercial and artisan activities, in particular metalworking. It also possessed a number of public spaces.

The most visible remains of Bibracte, and of all the oppida that have survived to the present day, are the fortifications. The *murus gallicus*, the 'Gallic wall' or rampart, is the most common type in central France and southern Germany. The ditch and earth ramparts typical of hillforts were reinforced by an elaborate system of interlacing timbers laid horizontally and fixed together with iron nails up to 30cm (1ft) long. The timbers were then filled with rubble and faced with dressed stone. They were extremely resistant to assault by undermining or by battering ram, and more difficult to scale than the sloping earth ramparts that were still a common feature of Belgic oppida north of the Loire and in southern Britain.

The oppidum of Bibracte was an important political and economic centre, channelling trade goods to and from the Roman south. Like other oppida in Gaul south of the Loire and in southern Germany, it had evolved rapidly from the latter half of the 2nd century BC. The reasons for the sudden appearance of these Celtic urban centres remain unclear. They were not merely a response to an external threat since not all of them were fortified, nor were they all sited on the basis of purely defensive or strategic considerations. It does seem likely, however, that political unrest was a significant factor in their emergence. The expansion of Rome into southern Gaul and the creation of the province of Gallia Transalpina, as well as the continuing consolidation of Roman conquests in Iberia, caused competition among Celtic tribes to intensify. Their efforts to satisfy Rome's ever-increasing need for raw materials led to conflict for control of trade networks. Manpower became a major commodity. Inter-tribal warfare was waged to procure captives to be sold as slaves, thousands of whom were required every year to maintain the labour force in Italy in the 1st century BC. The subsequent seizure of land resulted in increased centralization as communities sought to defend themselves, and in the abandonment of the former custom of collective ownership of the land in favour of a system of private property.

The development of a monetary-based economy and the growth of direct trading links with the Mediterranean had a substantial impact on Celtic society. The aristocratic elite were no longer so concerned with the pursuit of military glory as a means to ensure and enhance their status. To a certain extent, parallels can be drawn with the Halstatt Princedoms of the early Iron Age, whose position and prestige were based on their control of the distribution of foreign trade goods.

Another view of the murus gallicus at the entrance to the oppidum of Bibracte, with defensive ditch. (Author's collection)

Aerial view of the fort
of Dun Connor, Ireland.
This type of settlement
is reminiscent of the
castros of north-western
Iberia. (Werner
Forman Archive)

Whereas the evidence of the wealth revealed in Halstatt tombs strongly suggests
a society ruled by a monarchy, by the time the 'city states' of Gaul had emerged,
the ancient responsibilities of Celtic kings as described in Irish myths and legends
had been divided among members of the nobility. This noble oligarchy, or 'senate',
still dominated the tribe through the assembly of freemen, but instead of electing
a king, every year they elected a magistrate, called a *vergobretos* in Gaul, who
oversaw everyday affairs. All important decisions continued to be submitted to the
senate while the entire assembly of freemen was consulted only on rare occasions.
The term of office of the *vergobretos* and the specific responsibilities of the nobles
were limited to one year. The former was also forbidden to travel outside the
territory of the tribe and could not stand for re-election. All these restrictions
were intended to prevent power being concentrated in the hands of one man.
Severe sanctions were imposed on anyone who by his prestige or actions
was judged to be seeking to achieve personal power. Celtillus, the father of
Vercingetorix, one of the greatest leaders of the Celtic resistance against Caesar in
Gaul, was accused of trying to restore the monarchy and become king of the
Arverni. Despite his large following among the Arvernian nobility, his attempted
coup failed and he was executed.

The insights we have into the structures of Celtic society from the tales of pre-
Christian Ireland and from Caesar's *Commentaries on the Gallic War* in the 1st century
BC represent two distinct stages in a long process of evolution: the archaic era that
reaches back to the Bronze Age past, and which has much in common with the

'heroic' age of Homeric legend in Mycenaean Greece, and the sophisticated city states emerging in Gaul which were ultimately prevented from developing into a fully urban civilization by Roman intervention. This evolution was by no means consistent throughout the Celtic world. Celtic oppida in southern Germany and Bohemia show little or no sign of Mediterranean contact at this time, suggesting that exposure to the 'civilized' cultures of Greece and Rome was not the driving force in their development. Only in southern Gaul, near the Mediterranean coast, did classical influences make themselves felt. In the 2nd century BC, the oppidum of Entremont, near Marseille, the principal settlement of the Saluvii, developed into a Greek-style town with masonry defences modelled on those of nearby Greek coastal cities.

At the eastern extremity of the Celtic world, the Galatians who settled in Asia Minor were closely observed by the Greeks who lived in close proximity to them and who had to suffer their depredations. As a result, a great deal is known about their social and political structures. Each of the three Celtic tribes that had crossed the Hellespont in the wake of the great expedition into the Balkans in 279 BC was divided into four clans headed by a chieftain called a *tetrarch* by the Greeks. These

Aerial view of the fort of Dun Aengus, Inishmore, Ireland. (Werner Forman Archive)

chieftains were assisted by three military advisers and a judge. Between them, the 12 clans appointed 300 'senators' to attend an annual assembly at a shrine called the *drunemeton*, literally 'the oak sanctuary'. The three tribes and their respective clans were too jealous of their own independence to achieve any semblance of unity. We know of only one failed attempt by a noble, Ortiagon, to unite the Galatians against the Romans in the early 2nd century BC, by which time the clan chieftains considered themselves to be kings in their own right.

The development of Celtic urban society in Gaul was abruptly halted in the mid-1st century BC by Caesar's invasion. Paradoxically, this society's very success made its downfall almost inevitable. The increasing concentration of power weakened Celtic society and made it more vulnerable to attack. Greater economic prosperity made the oppida in Gaul and southern Germany a tempting target not only to Rome, but also to other peoples whose societies were less developed. By seizing the oppida, the surrounding territories would also fall. Caesar's campaigns in Gaul are, to a certain extent, concentrated around a series of sieges. In targeting the centres of elite power, the oppida, he ensured that he was able effectively to subdue the entire country in six years, until the revolt led by Vercingetorix broke out in 52 BC (see pp.163–71). Rome had far greater difficulty in conquering regions that were still politically and economically decentralized, such as Iberia or northern Britain, where effective control took decades or even longer to achieve.

WARFARE AND SOCIETY

War affected and conditioned the organization of the entire Celtic social, economic and religious system, just as war's own development was conditioned by the characteristics of the society.

Stable occupation of the land from the late Bronze Age onwards and differences in access to the means of production introduced social differences that were accentuated by the appearance of a class of skilled artisans. With the spread of private ownership of land and the development of the client system, larger and more cohesive social units began to be formed. The most powerful of these units produced aristocratic warrior lineages who sought to extend their influence by acquiring clients. The social and economic structure of early Celtic society was therefore a determining factor in imbuing it with a warrior ethos. War constituted the primary means of achieving prestige and wealth. The frequent raids organized against neighbouring tribes and territories and later service as mercenaries can be understood in this context. The expansion of these warrior groups encouraged a process of progressive 'Celticization'

The magnificent Agris helmet restored from the fragments found in western France. Made of iron, it is gold plated with silver, bronze and coral decoration. Dated to the late 4th century BC. (Musée de la Société archéologique et historique de la Charente / Bridgeman Art Library)

that would have forced other peoples to adopt a similar way of life as the best means of defence. This helps to explain the spread of Celtic warrior society from the end of the 5th century BC. Even before the period of the great Celtic migrations, the Celts practised ritual emigration, with expeditions lasting until the participants had decided to settle or had been killed in the attempt. Young men of military age devoted themselves to raiding and war in territories far away from their native communities.

This way of life, typical of pre-urban societies, contributed to the instability of Celtic society, and also explains its capacity for expansion, sometimes over large distances.

War in Celtic society also had a sacred and magical character. To be admitted to the warrior brotherhood, an individual would have to undergo initiation rites in order to prove his courage and commitment. Young Celtiberian warriors had to demonstrate aggression by cutting off the hands or heads of prisoners. The warrior groups were led by the chieftains, who would have been the most powerful and experienced among them, and who had demonstrated their ability to lead successful and profitable campaigns. In Iberia, warriors swore sacred oaths to the chieftains to follow them to the death, a practice known as *devotio*. Opposing warrior groups settled conflicts by a heroic combat between two champions whose fate decided that of their respective forces. Such combats are also documented in the legends of the Trojan War in Homer's *Iliad*. This ideological framework explains the special relationship of the Celts and especially the Celtiberians with their weapons. Literary sources frequently mention the warrior's refusal to surrender his arms, preferring death instead, as shown by the practice of committing suicide in accordance with devotio, which demanded that a warrior could not outlive his leader in battle. Cicero claimed that the Celtiberians delighted in battle and lamented if they were ill. Death in combat was glorious for the Celtiberians, and this is shown by the fact that those who fell in combat were rewarded with a specific funerary ritual: the exposure of the corpse to be devoured by vultures, which were considered sacred and entrusted with taking the deceased to the 'Otherworld', where he would share in the feast of the gods. The rich warrior graves found elsewhere throughout the Celtic world, complete with a panoply of arms, can in many cases perhaps be interpreted in the same way: as the burial of a famous warrior who died in battle.

Interestingly, from the middle of the 2nd century BC, weapons no longer appeared in tombs. A possible reason is that, in an age of intensifying war with Rome, the need for weapons made it necessary to abandon the custom of deposition of weapons in tombs. However, the evolution of an urban Celtic society seems a more logical explanation. Weapons would lose much of their symbolic value if social status depended less on war than on wealth. Their absence could therefore be related to the appearance of oppida from the end of the 3rd century BC.

The periodic raids that Celtic warrior groups made into neighbouring territories can be understood as a way of gaining prestige, social status and wealth. The same motives impelled them to fight as mercenaries in the armies of the Mediterranean powers, where their warlike skills were much valued. Celts served as mercenaries mainly before and after the confrontation with Rome, when the Celtic world was

reaching its apogee and was not yet itself under threat. Mercenaries were not individual soldiers of fortune, but well-organized groups of warriors. Through mercenary contact with the Greeks, Carthaginians and Romans, tribal forces became larger and better organized until they could be considered real armies. The armies would still be led by charismatic chieftains revered by their followers through devotio.

The concept of war underwent important changes as the Celts came into direct contact with the Mediterranean world. In the evolution toward a Celtic urban society, torcs, the famous Celtic neck rings, other jewellery and fine metalwork replaced weapons as status symbols. Earlier traditions still survived, however. One tradition was that of the warrior brotherhoods, which adapted to an urban environment. Another was the continued existence of the tribal military structure, as shown by the absence of standardized weapons and discipline, rather than the development of a true citizen army like those of the Roman Republic or the hoplite armies of the Greek city states. The nature of Celtic warfare changed from small-scale feuding between family groups and neighbouring communities to large conflicts between tribal confederations and the life and death struggle against Roman domination. The Celtic urban centres were ruled by the most powerful clans, which constantly sought to increase their power and territory. A major consequence was the increasing importance of cavalry as the preferred tactical arm of the Celtic noble elite, who were now comparable to the *equites*, the 'knightly' class of the Roman Republic. Their interests and concerns were no longer those of the warrior hero. These differences help explain the seemingly ambivalent attitude of many Celtic political leaders during the Gallic War.

Solid gold torcs from Britain, 1st century BC. On the left is the famous Snettisham torc. (Werner Forman Archive / British Museum, London)

CHAPTER 4

SHADOWS – ILLUSIVE IMAGES OF THE CELTIC GODS

The Gauls all claim to be descended from the god Dis Pater, saying that this tradition has been handed down by the Druids. (Caesar, The Conquest of Gaul)

Celtic religion remains a constant source of mystery and fascination. Images of Druid rituals and of human sacrifice deep in forest clearings are still those which most often come to mind. The fact that the ancient Celts never recorded details of their belief systems only serves to reinforce this. Yet there is perhaps more available evidence for Celtic religious belief than for any other aspect of Celtic culture. We are again reliant upon the accounts of classical writers and the vernacular literature of the Insular Celts of Wales and Ireland from the early Middle Ages. As always, such sources must be treated with caution. Caesar's account in his description of Gallic society in the 1st century BC, although comprehensive, provides only a snapshot of conditions that existed at a particular time and in a particular place. Ancient Welsh and Irish myths and legends must be viewed in the context of the Christian monastic environment through which they have come down to us. It is unlikely that Celtic religion was consistent throughout Europe in the later Iron Age, nor was it fixed and unchanging.

In recent years, the discovery and excavation of religious structures such as shrines and sanctuaries, together with the study of burial customs, ritual behaviour and iconography, have produced a greater understanding and insight into Celtic religious practices. The only first-hand testimony that we possess is in Celtic art. Potentially the most revealing, it is inevitably subject to widely differing interpretations. We are left, therefore, with only a fragmentary and distorted image of the spiritual world of the Celts from the available sources. Neither have we any idea how this world may have evolved. The situation is further complicated by the influence of older belief systems,

Detail of a bronze
statuette from northern
France possibly
representing a divinity,
1st century BC or AD.
The hairstyle and lack
of facial hair suggests
Mediterranean influence.
(The Art Archive /
Musée des Antiquités
nationales, St Germain-
en-Laye / Dagli Orti)

the immense diversity of the Celtic world, the relative isolation of some regions and the impact of social and economic change brought about by contact with the classical civilizations of the Mediterranean world. Nevertheless, despite the mass of disparate evidence, a number of broad similarities can be detected that enable us to reconstruct some semblance of the religious beliefs of the Celts.

The evidence we possess almost certainly relates to only a small part of the Celtic pantheon, probably the gods most venerated by the social elite, and in particular the warrior aristocracy. The Celts worshipped many gods and goddesses, of whom the names of over 200 have been preserved. A number of individual deities seem to have been revered throughout the Celtic world. Their functions were first described by Caesar in comparison with their Roman equivalents. Unfortunately, he did not list their Celtic names. Mercury was apparently the most honoured as 'the inventor of all arts'. Then came Apollo 'who averts disease', Mars 'the lord of war', Jupiter 'who rules the heavens' and Minerva 'who instructs in industry and craft'. The Roman poet Lucan named three gods to whom the Gauls offered human sacrifices: Teutates, whose victims were drowned, Taranis, whose victims were burnt, and Esus, to whom victims were sacrificed by hanging. Teutates was probably a generic term meaning 'god of the tribe', from the Celtic word *teuta* meaning 'tribe' or 'people'. He is identified with Mars,

Bronze yoke fitting featuring a female deity from Waldalgesheim, Germany. Dated to the 4th century BC. (akg-images / Erich Lessing)

Stone sculpture from Alésia of the horse goddess Epona.
(C. M. Dixon / Ancient Art & Architecture Collection Ltd)

to whom, according to Caesar, the Gauls consecrated their spoils of war. Taranis, whose name comes from the Celtic word for thunder, *taran*, was probably a god of the heavens and can be equated with Caesar's Jupiter. His symbol was the wheel. Esus means 'good' or 'capable' and is linked with Mercury. He has also been equated with Lugos or Lugh, called the 'Shining' and 'Many-skilled' in Irish myth. Through Irish legend we know of the Dagda, the 'good god' who protected the tribe and at the same time fulfilled the functions of giver of wisdom and lord of battle. His female counterpart was the Morrigan, often referred to as the 'Queen of Darkness', the

Stone figurine from
Gaul. The prominence
of the boar suggests the
shape-shifting ability
of many Celtic deities.
(Ancient Art
& Architecture
Collection Ltd)

goddess of fertility and destruction. Overlaying this ancient duality are deities such as Brigid, the 'Exalted', the daughter of the Dagda, and Lugh who shared many of the Dagda's skills. Both Brigid and Lugh were widely revered in Britain, Gaul and Iberia. Their arrival in the pantheon of Irish gods is a possible indication of the gradual Celticization of Ireland. Caesar's Dis Pater, known in Irish myth as Donn, 'the Dark Lord', was the mirror image of Lugh, 'the Lord of Light'. This balancing of complementary opposites is reflected in the pairing of two heads, which is a recurring theme in Celtic art.

The names of other Celtic gods are known from inscriptions of the Roman period and also from place names: for example, Belenos, another name for the sun god in Gaul; Camulos, a war god in Britain and Gaul whose name was preserved in Camulodunum, the oppidum of the Trinovantes, the modern-day Colchester; Cernunnos, the horned god and lord of the animal kingdom, whose origins are said to reach back to the Stone Age; and Epona, the Gallic horse goddess. Lugh gave his name to several European cities, including Lyon in France, Leiden in the Netherlands and Lugo in Spain. Some gods were associated with specific locations, in particular natural springs and other watercourses: Sulis was the goddess of the hot springs at Bath in Somerset, while Sequana was the goddess of the source of the river Seine in France, regarded by the Gauls as an especially holy place. Many, perhaps most, Celtic gods were simply local deities whose names have seldom been preserved. The difficulty faced by the Romans in attempting to equate the gods of the Celts with their own was compounded by the absence of any firm image of the divine. The role of the image was not intended to represent the real world, but to illustrate the hidden workings behind it. Unlike the Mediterranean peoples, the Celts did not envisage their deities in human form, at least not until the end of the 2nd century BC, when classical influence began to make itself felt in Celtic religious iconography. Diodorus Siculus tells of the astonishment of Brennus when he stood before the statues of the Greek gods in the great sanctuary at Delphi in 279 BC: 'When he came upon images of stone and wood, he laughed at them, to think that men believed that the gods had human form.' (*Historical Library*)

One of the characteristics of some Celtic deities at least was the ability to change their appearance at will. The prevalence of shape-shifting and zoomorphism (the portrayal of gods and men in animal form) emphasizes the important place that these creatures occupied in Celtic religious belief and acknowledges the subtle complexity of Celtic reality. Certain birds and animals held a particular significance for Celtic warriors and were revered for their specific qualities, such as valour, speed, ferocity and fidelity. Most common among the respected creatures were the bull, the horse, the wild boar, the raven and the dog. By adopting the symbol of the creature on his arms or armour, or in his appearance, the warrior, in his mind, would be endowed with these same qualities.

The everyday world of men and the Otherworld of the gods and the dead existed side by side. The line dividing the one from the other was blurred and ill-defined. The story of the warrior hero who strays unwittingly into the Otherworld while pursuing some enchanted beast is a common theme in Welsh and Irish legend. The Otherworld was perceived as being very much like that of mortal men but without pain, disease or old age. In Irish myth it was called *Tir na n'Og*, the land of eternal youth, and was regarded as a place of peace and beauty. In Welsh legend it was known as *Annwn*. Pwyll, the legendary Lord of Dyfed, is said to have dwelt there for a year, saying that 'Of all the courts he had seen on earth, it was the best-furnished with meat and drink, and with vessels of gold and royal jewels.' (Gantz, *Mabinogion*)

Here, Pwyll is alluding to a central feature of the Otherworld: the heroes' feast around the magic cauldron that, when emptied, would miraculously refill itself by the following day. Yet, for all its peace, beauty and wealth, the Otherworld was an ambiguous place, full of shadows and hidden menace. Mortal time had no meaning there. Anyone who had the misfortune to pass through the veil by accident, or who was foolish enough to accept an invitation from a supernatural creature in human disguise, would discover to his despair on returning home that in his one night of feasting a lifetime had passed.

THE DRUIDS

Philosophers and men learned in religious affairs are unusually honoured among them, and are called Druids. (Diodorus Siculus, *Historical Library*)

Linking the world of men and the Otherworld of the gods were the Druids. Their name is related to the Celtic word for oak tree (*drus*) and is possibly derived from an Indo-European root word meaning 'strong' and 'knowledge'. It appears in Old Irish as *drui* and in Welsh as *dryw*, meaning 'magician' and 'seer'. Although classical texts refer to them only in Britain and Gaul, it is probable that an equivalent priestly class existed elsewhere in the Celtic world. The clan chieftains of the Galatians are said to have been assisted by judges who may have fulfilled a similar role.

Bronze statuette
of a boar from Bohemia.
To the Celtic warrior, the
boar symbolized power,
strength and courage.
(Werner Forman
Archive / National
Museum, Prague)

Druid origins are obscure, although references to Druids in Irish myths and legends would seem to indicate that they existed as a priestly class in early Celtic society before the Migration Period. Caesar gives the fullest account of the Druids with whom he had contact in Gaul in the 1st century BC. He noted that all men of dignity and rank in Gaul were included among either the nobility or the Druids. They enjoyed high status as privileged members of the tribal elite and were exempt from taxation and military obligations. They were the guardians of tribal tradition and the administrators of tribal law as well as mediators with the gods:

The Druids officiate at the worship of the gods, regulate public and private sacrifice, and rule on all religious questions. A great number of young men gather about them for the sake of instruction and hold them in great honour. It is they who decide in almost all public and private disputes, and if any crime has been committed or murder done, or if there is any dispute over succession or boundaries, they also decide it, determining rewards and penalties.
(Caesar, *The Conquest of Gaul*)

The authority of the Druids was both spiritual and civil, and extended from individuals to whole tribes. Druids were closely involved in politics and diplomacy. They oversaw the taking of oaths and were almost certainly responsible for the imposition of taboos and rules (geissi). They also had the power of excommunication, banning people from taking part in sacrifice and other public ceremonies, effectively removing their religious and legal status. According to Caesar, this was the heaviest punishment that could be inflicted on a Gaul. Such individuals were shunned as unclean.

One of the main tenets of the philosophy of the Druids was the transmigration of the soul, the belief that the soul did not die, but passed from one body to another after death. This belief led a number of ancient writers to the conclusion that the Druids might have been influenced by the teachings of the Greek philosopher Pythagoras. However, such is most likely to be the natural assumption of the 'civilized' Mediterranean world when confronted with so-called barbarians who were found to have similar beliefs.

Caesar wrote that the Druids in Gaul elected one of their number to lead their order for life. They met once a year in a sacred grove of oak trees in the territory of the Carnutes, which was considered to be the centre of Gaul. The concept of 'the centre' is one that was of particular significance to the Celts' view of the universe, and is one which we will explore further (see p.103). It is probably no coincidence that the assembly of the Galatians was known as the drunemeton, 'oak sanctuary'. The purpose of the gathering was to debate and decide on all major issues. It is likely that the decision to resist Caesar's efforts to crush Gallic opposition to Roman rule was taken during one such gathering. Likewise, it may be no coincidence that the rebellion of Boudica in Britain a century later began following the destruction of the holiest of Druid sanctuaries on Mona (Anglesey).

As in other pre-literate cultures, Druidic lore and learning were passed on orally, using poetic metre and rhyme to commit them to memory. When the Celts began to adopt alphabets from the Mediterranean world, it was forbidden to commit this knowledge to writing. It was said that training to become a Druid took up to 20 years. It is likely, therefore, that novices, who were chosen from the nobility, began their studies at the same age as other children were fostered into the families of patrons. In Irish legend, Cathbad, the chief Druid at the court of Conchobar, king of Ulster, is accompanied by a number of youths who wish to learn his art. Caesar also noted that many aspiring Druids travelled to Britain, where the best instruction was to be found. The important Druidic centre on Mona may be connected with this.

According to other classical authors, the Celtic priestly class also included seers or soothsayers, and bards. The former, known in Latin as *vates* from a Celtic word meaning 'inspired' or 'ecstatic', were described by Strabo as diviners and natural philosophers. They were said to foretell the future by means of the flight and cries of birds and the sacrifice of sacred animals. As we have seen, bards were the repositories of the myths and legends of the Celtic peoples. At the feasts and festivals of the Celtic year they sang the songs recalling the great deeds of the warrior heroes and recounting the genealogies and family histories of the noble elite.

There is no evidence to suggest the existence of female Druids. Priestesses, however, are mentioned in Gaul and Britain. Strabo mentions a community of Gallic priestesses who lived in isolation on an island near the estuary of the Loire. They were said to reconsecrate their dwelling every year in a ceremony during which one of their number was sacrificed by being torn apart by her sisters. In Britain, the terrifying appearance and screaming curses of the priestesses unnerved the Romans under Agricola as they prepared to set foot on the island of Mona. The only female Druid known with any certainty was the legendary Scarthach to whom Cúchulainn was sent to be initiated into the way of the warrior.

The Druids in general were regarded with fear and loathing by the Romans, who professed themselves to be horrified by their custom of human sacrifice. While it cannot be denied that human sacrifice was an important factor in Celtic religion, the Romans were hardly in a position to point the finger at others when they did not hesitate to resort to similar practices themselves. The real reason behind the revulsion was almost certainly the power that the Druids wielded in Celtic society, a power that could provide a focus for resistance and rebellion against Roman interests, as happened in Gaul and Britain. The Emperor Augustus forbade Roman citizens to practise Druidical rites. Under his successor Tiberius, the Druids in Gaul were suppressed. A similar attempt was made in Britain after the Claudian invasion, with mixed results, as Agricola was to discover. In Ireland, Druids maintained their position and influence in society until their status was undermined by the arrival of Christianity.

The traditional association of Druids with Stonehenge has no basis in reality. It was first made in the 16th century as an attempt to explain the mysteries of this and other great stone circles in Britain. These prehistoric monuments, which date from the late Neolithic and Bronze Ages, were abandoned long before the evolution of Celtic culture. Neither is there any evidence that Stonehenge was ever used by Druids in the late Iron Age. Nevertheless, today it has become an important site for modern spiritual movements inspired by the ancient Druids.

Stone heads reminiscent
of the Roman twin-
headed god Janus from
the Saluvian sanctuary
at La Roquepertuse,
3rd to 2nd century BC.
(The Art Archive /
Musée d'Archéologie
méditerranéenne,
Marseilles / Dagli Orti)

GIFTS TO THE GODS

They used to shoot men down with arrows, impale them in temples or make a large statue of
straw and wood, and throw into it all sorts of cattle, wild animals and human beings, thus
making a burnt offering. (Strabo, *Geography*)

Several classical authors wrote about the practice of human sacrifice among the
Celts. Lucan described the methods preferred by Taranis, Teutates and Esus, while
Strabo repeated Poseidonius' account quoted above, which gave rise to the popular
image of the wicker man in which groups of unfortunates were burned to death.
Caesar also mentions this, probably referring to the same source. In Britain, Tacitus
tells of victims sacrificed on 'the blood-soaked altars' of Mona, while Boudica
impaled captives taken during the rebellion of the Iceni, though it is not clear
whether this was done as an offering to the gods or as an act of revenge. The Galatoi
of Asia Minor were held in dread because of their reputation for sacrificing prisoners
of war, and enemies would prefer to commit suicide rather than fall into their hands.
Caesar wrote that offerings to the gods included warriors taken in battle: '[the
Gauls] who are engaged in the perils of battle either sacrifice human victims or vow
to do so, employing Druids as ministers, for they believe that unless a man's life is
paid for another's, the majesty of the gods may not be appeased.'

Caesar's comment emphasizes the ritual nature of the sacrifice. It was no mere crude butchery. It had its allotted place in the belief system of the Celts and served a specific purpose for the warrior. The sacrifice represented a gift of something of value; the greater the value of the gift, the more powerful was the act of propitiation. In offering a captive for sacrifice, the warrior fulfilled his vow made to the gods in the presence of the Druids and at the same time enhanced his status in both this world and the Otherworld. Human sacrifice served not only to propitiate the gods, but also as a method of divination:

> They devote to death a human being and stab him with a dagger in the region of the chest. When he has fallen they foretell the future from the manner of his fall and from the convulsions of his limbs and from the spurting of his blood, placing their trust in an ancient and long continued observation of these practices. (Diodorus Siculus, *Historical Library*)

Archaeological evidence for human sacrifice among the Celts is hard to identify. Perhaps the clearest indication is the body discovered in a bog in Cheshire, England. Dubbed 'Lindow Man' after the site where he was found, he had been

Wooden bucket with bronze fittings, from a grave at Aylesbury, Buckinghamshire, possibly representing the magic cauldron of Celtic myth, 1st century BC. (The Art Archive / The British Museum)

strangled, struck on the head and had his throat cut in rapid succession. His state of health, the care taken with his appearance (he had manicured nails) and the traces of mistletoe found in his stomach give the impression that this was no ordinary sacrifice. Mistletoe was highly regarded by the Druids for its medicinal and other properties, especially since it grew on oak trees. In the case of Lindow Man, it could have been used as a drug to sedate him or perhaps to induce an altered state of consciousness as part of the ritual.

It was not unheard of for individuals to volunteer for such a fate in order to become the bearer of an important message to the gods. Although there are very few allusions to human sacrifice in Celtic vernacular literature, in Irish tradition a king would be ritually killed at *Samhain*, the modern Halloween, the time of year when the barrier between the world of men and the Otherworld vanished almost entirely.

The custom of dedicating gifts to the gods, especially trophies taken in war, as well as the taboo associated with them, is illustrated in ancient texts and by archaeological finds:

> When the Gauls decide to wage war, they dedicate the spoils they hope to win to Mars. If they are victorious, they sacrifice the captured animals and collect all the other spoils in one place. Among many tribes it is possible to see piles of these objects on holy ground. No man dares to go against religious law and conceal or remove any of the objects that have been placed there. The punishment decreed for such a crime is death under torture. (Caesar, *The Conquest of Gaul*)

The great treasure at Tolosa (Toulouse) can be considered in this context. Believed to have come originally from the sack of Delphi by Brennus, part was kept in sacred enclosures while other objects had been thrown into nearby lakes. Revered by the Celtic inhabitants of the region, it remained protected by their religious taboos until it was looted by the Romans in 107 BC. Interestingly, the Roman commander, Caepio, suffered a series of misfortunes thereafter and never profited from the pillage

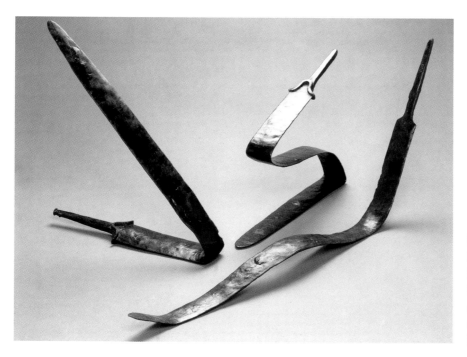

Sword blades 'ritually killed' as votive offerings, from the sanctuary at Gournay-sur-Aronde in northern France, late 3rd century BC. (akg-images / Pietro Baguzzi)

of the sanctuary. Whether or not the figure of 50 tonnes (49 tons) of gold from the treasure at Toulouse can be credited, the scale of the ritual deposits of the Celts was substantial. Caesar was apparently able to clear his debts and finance his future career with his share of the spoils from the war in Gaul.

The Celts regarded watercourses as a powerful manifestation of the supernatural, perhaps through their intimate connection with the earth and as a way of reaching the Otherworld. The dying Arthur was taken across the lake to be made whole again in Avalon, while his sword, Excalibur, was cast into the water. The site at La Tène, the name of which characterizes the material culture of the Celts in the later Iron Age, is also believed to be a place where objects were ritually offered to the gods. Llyn Cerrig Bach on the Druids' holy island of Anglesey and the site of the modern city of Geneva are further examples of such ritual sites where objects were cast into lakes. Large quantities of weapons have been discovered in European rivers. In Britain, several rich finds have been recovered from the Thames, the most well known being the Battersea (see p.119) and Wandsworth shields and the famous horned helmet found near Waterloo Bridge (see pp.142–3). Reverence for springs was also widespread. The shrine of Sequana at the source of the river Seine in Burgundy was

Source of a tributary of the river Seine. The Celts regarded watercourses as a powerful manifestation of the supernatural. This site is still a place of veneration over 2,000 years later. (Author's collection)

one of the most important in Gaul. Belief in the healing power of the water and the goddess is shown by the symbolism of the substantial number of votive offerings that have been found there. These take the form of small wooden figurines emphasizing certain parts of the body. The thermal springs of the goddess Sulis at Bath can also be considered in this context. The majority of these water sites are dedicated to female deities. This is in line with the general Celtic belief in the feminine nature of the earth, which has come down to us today in the folklore of holy wells associated with female Christian saints.

It is clear from the archaeological record that the Celts felt the need to appease their gods not only in time of war, which would have been the responsibility of the noble elite and the warrior caste, but also in their everyday lives. In a society reliant upon successful harvests year after year, ensuring the benevolence of the gods was of vital importance. Evidence of this effort is revealed in the offerings placed in pits used to store grain. Once the grain had been removed and sown, a propitiatory offering was made, most commonly of domestic animals but sometimes of human bodies, in whole or in part, including severed heads. Animal bodies included sheep, cattle and pigs – animals of value as food – as well as others such as horses and dogs, whose worth would have had a more ritual significance. These offerings appear to have been made in two stages: in spring at the time of sowing and later in the summer at the time of harvest, perhaps corresponding with particular seasonal festivals. Poor harvests may have required a special offering in the form of a human sacrifice. Pastoral communities, particularly in Ireland and Scotland, which were more dependent on flocks and herds than on agriculture, tended to make their offerings to the gods in bogs.

The desire to appease the gods of the earth is also apparent in the practice of digging ritual shafts deep into the ground. The tradition is an ancient one dating back to the Bronze Age, although the majority of Celtic examples have been dated to the last two centuries BC. Many of them are located within rectangular ditched enclosures known by the German term *Viereckschanzen*, which have been found throughout Celtic Europe from Britain to Bohemia. Although the function of the enclosures remains unclear, many of the shafts contained a variety of votive offerings. At Holzhausen in Bavaria, three shafts 2.5m (8ft 2in) across and 40m (131ft 3in) deep were discovered together with a timber structure believed to be a shrine. At the bottom of one of the shafts, an upright wooden stake was found to have traces of flesh and blood on it. Human and animal bones as well as wooden figures and pottery vessels have been found in similar shafts elsewhere in Germany and France, where their use continued into the Roman period.

PAGE 99: Detail of one of the panels of the Gundestrup cauldron. The image of Cernunnos, 'the horned man', suggests the shamanistic symbolism of the union between man and the creatures of the wild, in particular the stag, which was venerated by the Celts for its strength and virility. The torc is clearly shown to be a ritual object, and it is perhaps significant that the figure clutches a serpent in its left hand, another symbol of fertility and regeneration. (Werner Forman Archive / National Museum, Copenhagen)

The 'Warrior' panel of the Gundestrup cauldron portrays warriors on horseback and on foot. None of the latter wear helmets except the figure on the right, armed with a sword, who appears to be the leader. The helmet crests on this figure and on the horsemen suggest animal totems: boar, raven, stag, bull and horse. The Celtic war horn, the *carnyx*, is clearly shown. The significance of the large figure on the left is uncertain: could it be a representation of rebirth via the symbolism of the cauldron itself, shown here, after death on the battlefield? (akg-images / Erich Lessing)

THE GUNDESTRUP CAULDRON

The remarkable vessel known as the Gundestrup cauldron was discovered in a peat bog near Gundestrup in Denmark in 1891. Consisting of a round base, five outer and seven inner plates, it has a diameter of 69cm (27¼in) and a height of 42cm (16½in). Its plates are made of almost pure silver. The figures on the outside of the vessel were originally covered with gold leaf with eyes set with red and blue glass. It is one of the most magnificent and most enigmatic relics of the Celtic world.

The cauldron is thought to date from the 2nd or 1st century BC. While much of the imagery is Celtic, the style and workmanship are characteristic of the non-Celtic Thracians who lived in eastern Europe, in present-day Bulgaria and Romania. This has given rise to conflicting theories for its origin. One possible explanation might be that the cauldron was produced by Thracian craftsmen for the Celtic Scordisci who dominated the middle Danube. How it came to be in Denmark is another unanswered question. It may have been passed on through an exchange of gifts or perhaps fell into the hands of the Cimbri when they raided the Scordisci during their migration south from Jutland across Europe at the end of the 2nd century BC.

The cauldron is decorated with scenes depicting Celtic deities and rituals, accompanied by motifs of plants and fantastic beasts. The scenes provide a unique glimpse into Celtic myth and legend, albeit one whose meaning remains elusive. Particularly striking are the representations of the ritual initiation of a group of warriors, the sacrifice of three bulls and a horned god usually interpreted as Cernunnos who

appears in other contexts in northern Gaul. It has also been suggested that the horned figure symbolizes Cúchulainn rather than Cernunnos, and even that the entire iconography of the Gundestrup cauldron can be viewed as a prototype of the Irish myth of the *Táin Bó Cuailnge*. Though this is only one theory among others, it is by no means unlikely that the images portrayed represent a coherent narrative.

SACRED TIME AND SACRED SPACE

Because the Druids did not commit their philosophy to writing, no record exists to explain how the Celts perceived their world. Classical authors and the myths and legends that have survived in Ireland and Wales give some information, while Celtic art reveals the frequent use of a number of common symbolic elements relating to time and space. An indication of how the Celts viewed the passing of time – crucial to the well-being of any agricultural society and to the correct performance of rituals which would ensure this – is provided by the calendar discovered in 1897 at Colligny near Lyon in south-eastern France.

The Colligny Calendar is made up of 73 surviving fragments of a series of bronze tablets. The engraved letters are Latin, but the language is Gaulish. By comparing it

Fragments of the Colligny Calendar. The letters and numbers are Latin but the language is Gaulish. Dated to the end of the 1st century AD. (Musée de la Civilisation Gallo-Romaine, Lyon)

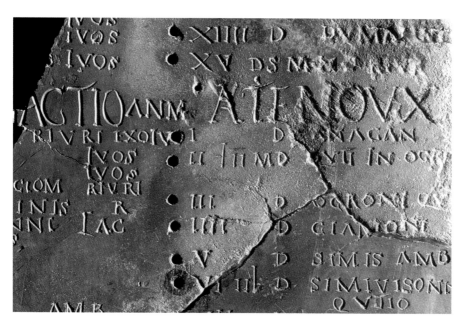

Detail of the Colligny Calendar. (Musée de la Civilisation Gallo-Romaine, Lyon)

with other finds excavated from the same site, it has been dated to the 1st century AD, a time when the Julian Calendar was being introduced throughout the Roman Empire. The Colligny Calendar was used for liturgical purposes in a sanctuary where traditional Celtic worship persisted. The calendar was 'lunisolar' and attempted to combine and reconcile the monthly cycles of the moon with the yearly cycle of the sun. This format is very old. An engraved stone found in Ireland and dated to the Neolithic period (before 2000 BC) has been interpreted as a representation of a lunar calendar that may have been developed on the same principles as the Colligny Calendar. The restored tablet has 16 vertical columns showing a five-year cycle consisting of 62 lunar months. According to this system, the lunar year contained 354 or 355 days. Each month was divided into a 'dark' and a 'light' half, which were the basic units of the Celtic calendar. The first half was always 15 days long; the second half had 14 or 15 days on alternate months. Months of 30 days were considered to be *matos* or auspicious, those of 29 days as *anmatos*, inauspicious. All months were deemed to begin at the time of the full moon. The solar year was brought back into line by the addition of a 13th month every two and a half years. Each year was also divided in two, the light half beginning around the end of April and the dark half around the end of October, depending on the time of the full moon. The new year began at the start of the dark half, during the 'three nights of *Samonios*', mentioned on the calendar and coinciding with the nearest full moon to the beginning of November. *Samonios* is usually assumed to correspond with the *Samhain* in Ireland.

Bronze mirror from Hereford of a type found only in late Iron Age Britain. Note the swirling 'S' pattern, symbolizing eternal regeneration, forming the triple spiral figure, or triskelion, one of the most enduring symbols in Celtic art. (Werner Forman Archive / British Museum, London)

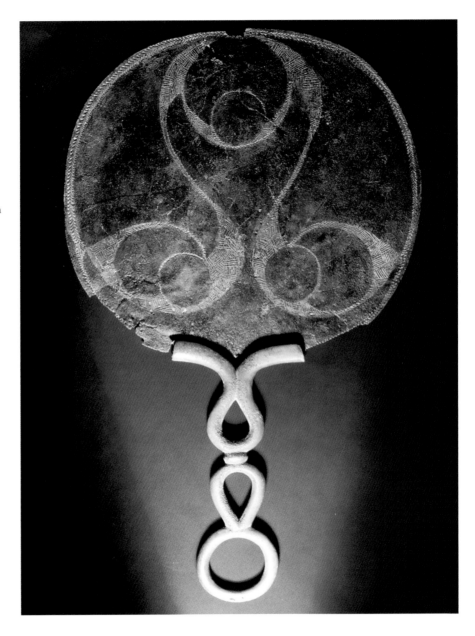

In Irish tradition, the four great festivals of the Celtic year were *Samhain*, *Imbolc*, *Beltane* and *Lughnasadh*. They correspond to Halloween, Candlemass at the beginning of February, May Day and the harvest season in north-west Europe at the beginning of August. The Colligny Calendar only refers to the first, although *Beltane*, marking the beginning of the other principal season of the year, is implied. Since none of the festivals has any connection with the summer and winter solstices nor with the spring and autumn equinoxes, it has been suggested that they were originally fixed by observation of certain stars that featured prominently at the respective times of the year. *Samhain* has been associated with the star Antares, in the constellation of Scorpio, and *Beltane* with Aldebaran, in the constellation of Taurus. The theory is supported by a Gallo-Roman zodiac inscribed on tablets found at the site of a sanctuary at Grand in Lorraine. This divides the year in two, one-half placed under the sign of the moon beginning with Scorpio and the other under the sign of the sun beginning with Taurus.

The division of time into two equal and complementary halves is symbolized by the swirling 'S' patterns that frequently occur in Celtic art. Signifying not only the apparent course of the sun throughout the year, but also its journey from east to west during the day and its return at night from west to east below the earth, the 'S' symbolizes eternal regeneration and represents the fundamental order of the universe. The movement of the sun from its rising through its zenith to its setting is also thought by some to be expressed in the triple-armed or triple spiral figure known as the triskelion. This is an ancient design that appears in many cultures. With the replacement of the geometric forms of the Halstatt period by the curvilinear La Tène style in the 5th and 4th centuries BC, the triskelion became one of the most important and enduring symbols in Celtic art.

The unending cycles of the sun through its daily east–west movement, and its north–south rising and falling throughout the year, also formed the basis for the Celts' spatial perception of the mortal world, which they saw as divided into four parts. In Celtic art this is represented by the solar wheel with its four axes intersecting at the centre. This symbolic centre had great significance for the Celts and formed the basis for many artistic compositions. Celtic Christian crosses still retain this combination of circle and cross. The concept of a fourfold space around a centre is illustrated by the traditional division of Ireland into four kingdoms, each of which contributed territory to a fifth, Midhe, the Middle Kingdom, where the High Kings of Ireland were crowned at Tara. The Galatoi of Asia Minor were divided into four tetrarchies; Caesar reported similar divisions among the Helvetii. Among many Celtic peoples the symbolic centre of their territories was known as *Mediolanon*, a term preserved in the name of the Italian city of Milan. The territory of the Carnutes was considered to be the ritual centre of Gaul where the annual gathering of the Druids was held.

Bronze belt buckle featuring two opposing double-headed creatures (horses?) with a human figure between them. A smaller creature at the base completes the threefold composition. (C. M. Dixon / Ancient Art & Architecture Collection Ltd)

Because of the association of the Druids with sacred groves of oak trees, it is often assumed that the Celts did not build temples or shrines, worshipping their gods in the open air. Archaeology, however, has revealed the existence of many enclosures and structures that have been interpreted as having a religious or ritual purpose. Nevertheless, the traditional image of Druids performing their ceremonies in forest glades has a basis in truth. Specific sacred locations in Gaul were known by the word *nemeton*, meaning a sacred clearing in a wood or a sacred grove. The term occurs throughout the Celtic world, from the *drunemeton* of the Galatians to *nemetobriga* of the Hispanic Celts and *aquae arnemetiae* in Britain. An evocative description of a sacred grove, in southern Gaul, and the reaction of Caesar to it is given by the Roman poet Lucan:

> The grove there was untouched by human hands from ancient times, whose interlacing boughs enclosed a space of darkness and cold shadow which banished the sunlight from above. Gods were worshipped there with savage rites, the altars heaped with hideous offerings, every tree sprinkled with human gore. Birds feared to perch on the branches, wild beasts would not lie down. No wind bore down upon that wood; the leaves of the trees rustled without a breeze. Water fell from dark springs. The grim images of the gods were uncouth blocks formed from felled tree trunks. Their age and the ghastly hue of the rotten timber struck terror. Legend told of underground hollows that quaked and groaned, of yew trees that fell and rose again, of flames that came from trees that were not on fire, and that serpents glided around their trunks. People never came there to worship but left the place to the gods. By day or night, even the priest dreads their approach and fears to come upon the lord of the grove. (*The Civil War*)

Caesar had it cut down, supposedly because it grew near his works. However, it is far more likely that he did so in order to destroy the power of the place and to demonstrate the superiority of Roman arms over the gods of the Celts.

Sanctuaries constructed by the Celts can be divided into two groups: the so-called Celto-Ligurian type common in southern France, and the purely Celtic type found in a broad zone extending from southern Germany across northern France to Britain. The former is characterized by the sites at La Roquepertuse and Entremont near the Mediterranean coast. The monumental style of their architecture reveals the influence of the Greeks of Massalia, but the carved stone heads and the niches reserved for the real thing, some still with holes for the nails to attach them, are completely and undeniably Celtic in nature (see p.106). In the northern zone, sanctuaries usually consisted of a rectangular or, in Britain, sometimes round, roofed timber structure within a sacred enclosure defined by a ditch and palisade. Those discovered at

Gournay-sur-Aronde and Ribemont-sur-Ancre in northern France offer a remarkable insight into the arrival of the Belgae in Gaul. Trophies dated to the mid-3rd century BC from battles between the newcomers and the local tribes, including the bodies of the victors and vanquished, were displayed until the flesh had rotted from the bones. These were then broken up and cast into the ditch, together with thousands of weapons, swords, spearheads and shield bosses that had been 'ritually killed' (see p.95).

THE CULT OF THE SEVERED HEAD

The Celts believed that the dwelling place of the immortal soul was the head: to possess an enemy's head was to possess his soul. As with many aspects of the warrior's life, the taking of an opponent's head in battle, preferably as a result of single combat, had a mystical significance. But it was this gruesome practice that was regarded as the most barbaric characteristic of the Celtic warrior by the Greeks and Romans, who were appalled at the desecration of the bodies of the dead on moral and religious grounds. Diodorus Siculus writes:

> When their enemies fall, they cut off their heads and fasten them to the bridles of their horses; and handing over to their retainers the arms of their opponents all covered with blood, they carry them off as booty, singing a song of victory. These first fruits of victory they nail to the sides of their houses just as men do in certain kinds of hunting with the heads of wild beasts they have killed. They embalm the heads of their most distinguished foes in cedar oil and carefully preserve them. They show them to visitors, proudly stating that they had refused a large sum of money for them. (*Historical Library*)

From this account we can conclude that, apart from being tangible proof of the courage and prowess of the warrior, the head of the fallen enemy became an important prestige object. The care in its preservation, the pride in its exhibition and the fact that it was considered to be of great value, perhaps implied a deeply felt bond between the victor and the vanquished. The importance and extent of the cult of

Stone head, perhaps of a Celtic god, found within a sacred enclosure in Bohemia. The Celts believed the head possessed great supernatural power: it was the centre of the spiritual being and repository of the soul. (Werner Forman Archive / Národni Museum, Prague)

Reconstruction of a stone portal from the sanctuary at La Roquepertuse showing skulls placed in niches. (akg-images / Erich Lessing)

the severed head among the Celts is demonstrated by the many examples of monumental carving found throughout the Celtic world and by the display of sculpted or human heads in shrines, either mounted in stonework, as at La Roquepertuse in southern Gaul, or on wooden poles as at the hillfort at Bredon Hill in western Britain. It is interesting to note that heads were often set up at entrances to defended sites. Perhaps the souls of these unfortunate warriors were being used to provide symbolic protection for their enemies' strongholds.

In Welsh and Irish myths, the severed head is imbued with supernatural power. When Bran the Blessed, one of the principal heroes in the Welsh legends of the *Mabinogion*, is mortally wounded in battle, he commands his own men to cut off his head and bury it in London where the White Tower now stands in the Tower of London, facing east to guard Britain against foreign invasion. Reverence for the power of the human head is also illustrated by Livy's account of a battle between the Romans and the Boii in the 3rd century BC. The Romans were defeated and the consul Postumus killed. His body was taken to the Boii's principal sanctuary where it was decapitated. The head was then cleaned and mounted with gold to be used as a cup in honour of the gods. The carved stone heads and the skulls found in the sanctuaries at La Roquepertuse and Entremont can be understood in this context.

DEATH AND REBIRTH

The wealth of evidence from the excavation of cemeteries indicates a widely held belief in an afterlife among the Celts. According to Caesar, the Druids believed that the soul passed from one body to another after death, and that this belief made Celtic warriors fearless in battle. The Druids' belief in the immortality of the soul is echoed by the cauldron of rebirth that often appears in Welsh and Irish myths. It had the power to restore warriors to life by immersing them in the water it contained. Interestingly, one of the main panels of the Gundestrup cauldron shows a supernatural being apparently plunging a figure into a sort of cauldron, while other Celtic warriors wait in line (see illustration p.98). Sacred cauldrons are recorded at a number of other Celtic sites, all associated with lakes or springs.

Throughout the later Iron Age the most common burial practice in the Celtic world was inhumation. Much of what we know about the Celts has come from the study of the grave goods that accompanied the dead. Many of the greatest surviving Celtic treasures have been discovered in cemeteries such as those at Vix and Hochdorf. Inhumation provided another opportunity to display status in the community. The burials of the Halstatt Princedoms in the 6th and 5th centuries BC

Chariot burial at Garton in East Yorkshire, 1st century BC. Note the items of metalwork placed with the body. (© Trustees of the British Museum / PS174448)

contained Greek and Etruscan prestige goods, which were obtained through Celtic control of major trade routes. From the beginning of the 4th century BC, status was expressed in terms of the warrior ethos with arms and armour, and in some areas even chariots featured in the richest burials. In Britain the majority of the dead, whether the noble elite or the unfree peasantry, are undetectable from an archaeological point of view except for the chariot burials in Yorkshire, which have been compared with those in the Marne area in France. It is thought that many were buried temporarily or exposed to the elements until the flesh had rotted from the body, a process called excarnation, after which the bones were removed, in whole or in part, to be used for further rituals. This practice may also explain the large number of dismembered skeletons carefully placed in the ritual pits and enclosures of the larger sanctuaries in northern Gaul. In Iberia, the Celtiberian Vaccaei fed the bodies of those who had died in war to vultures, believing the bird to be sacred, just as the crow and raven were revered elsewhere in the Celtic world.

Towards the end of the 2nd century BC, a change in burial practice from inhumation to cremation can be detected across much of Celtic Europe. This may indicate a change in belief or simply the adoption of the Mediterranean custom. It coincided with the sudden decline of warrior graves in areas where inhumation continued. Luxury items, especially gold torcs and wine *amphorae*, replaced weapons in the display of status. The evolution of Celtic society in direct contact with the Mediterranean world is almost certainly a factor here. One of the consequences of the increasing urbanization of much of the Celtic world was the reduced emphasis placed by the ruling elite on the way of the warrior.

CHAPTER 5

THE WAY OF THE WARRIOR

Rise kings of Macha/modest people   *lords and princes/lead in battle*
of mighty acts/blades are battering   *or end in blood/a forest of men*
battle raging/the earth torn up   *where they march or fall/bitter blood drained*
shields beaten/arms weary   *hearts of queens/filled with grief*
herds bellowing/in the rightful fight   *the dire advance/grass soaked with blood*
battle ranks trampled/underfoot   *where they stand and fall/rise kings of Macha*
                                              (Kinsela, Táin Bó Cuailnge)

THE WARRIOR HERO

All the evidence that we possess about the Celts indicates that warfare was crucial to their culture and to the maintenance of the structure of their society. The weapons that are characteristic of elite male graves in the La Tène period demonstrate that the warrior aristocracy was one of the most important elements in this social system. Ancient Irish myths describe a society dominated by the warrior hero. In many ways the society was similar to that of Mycenaean Greece as described by Homer. Glory on the field of battle was the sole aim of the Celtic warrior, who dreamed of following the example set by the heroes of legend. The glorious deeds of warriors, living or dead, that were retold at the feast instilled an acute sense of honour and laid down certain rules of conduct for the warrior throughout his life: a victory gained dishonestly was more degrading than a defeat suffered at the hands of a stronger adversary; it was unthinkable that a warrior should die other than in battle. Each warrior was also subject to personal taboos known as *geissi*, constraints on his free will that he must obey or defy at his peril.

As mentioned previously, clans and tribes were in a constant state of conflict. The fundamental role that livestock played in the establishment of Celtic social hierarchy made cattle rustling a prime cause of aggression. In the Ulster Cycle of ancient Irish tales, the central episode in the *Táin* is concerned with the bloody conflict that resulted from a simple marital quarrel over personal prestige and the subsequent theft of the brown bull of Cooley coveted by Medb, queen of Connaught (Shakespeare's Queen Mab), to rival the white bull owned by her husband Ailill. In this epic struggle, Cúchulainn fulfils the archaic role of the warrior hero as tribal champion and defender of the territory.

The Leinster Cycle of Irish myths and legends presents a different view of the Celtic warrior. Here he is personified by the *fianna*, a following or retinue of young men of noble descent who no longer form part of the traditional framework of the tribal community. Led by the hero Finn, they lived on the margins of society, wandering through Ireland offering their services as mercenaries to kings and chieftains. The fianna respected the warrior's code of honour, but regarded war as an end in itself, breaking the link with a particular tribal territory.

The ideal of a life dedicated to war and ending in a good death in battle to join the ranks of the immortal heroes in the Otherworld is also well illustrated by the Gaesatae at the battle of Telamon. This type of warrior ideology probably corresponds to the situation that existed among the continental Celts during the migrations of the 4th and 3rd centuries BC and was perhaps a factor in the downfall of the Halstatt Princedoms a century earlier. Such mobile groups operating outside the traditional tribal system were almost certainly the principal driving force behind the expansion of the Celts during this period. The warrior hosts which took part in the Great Expedition to the Balkans and those who later settled in western Europe can be compared to the fianna of Ireland. They formed new communities outside the traditional tribal system that were based on confederations of diverse ethnic groups organized on military lines. The Galatoi of Asia Minor, the Belgae and the Allobroges are all good examples of such groups. The heroic ideal of the Celtic warrior remained a potent force among the aristocracy that dominated the Celtic city states which emerged in the last two centuries BC, even after the settlement of these communities. However, the efforts made by the ruling oligarchies to prevent the usurpation of power by charismatic individuals are an indication that the 'old ways' were still a force to be reckoned with. The execution of Celtillus, a nobleman of the Arverni who was accused of attempting to restore the monarchy and make himself king, can be considered in this

Bronze statue of a naked Celtic warrior. Note the details of the horned helmet, torc and sword belt. The sword and shield are lost. Found in Italy, it could perhaps be a representation of the Gaesatae. (akg-images / Erich Lessing)

light. Ironically, it was his son, Vercingetorix, who was later to be proclaimed leader of all the Gallic tribes in the rebellion against Caesar in 52 BC.

APPEARANCE AND DRESS

The appearance of the Celts seemed strange and outlandish to the Greeks and Romans. Diodorus Siculus gives a vivid description:

> The Gauls are tall of body, with rippling muscles, and white of skin. Their hair is fair, not only by nature but also because of their custom of accentuating it by artificial means. They wash their hair in lime water then pull it back so that it resembles a horse's mane. Some of them shave their beard, others let it grow. The nobles shave their cheeks but let their moustache grow until it covers their mouth. (*Historical Library*)

This bronze statuette from central Gaul, dated to the late 1st century AD, gives an indication of how a Celtic noble may have looked. (akg-images / Erich Lessing)

The reference to fair hair and pale skin contrasts with the description of some present-day Celts such as the Welsh and Bretons who are viewed as having dark hair and matching complexions. It merely reinforces the fact that the Celts have always been a group of peoples linked by culture and language rather than a distinct race. Despite their reputation for being tall, archaeological remains seem to indicate that the average height for a Celt was 1.7m (5ft 7in). The average height for Romans, however, was several centimetres shorter.

The reference to lime-washed hair is interesting in the light of the spiritual symbolism of the horse. Such a style was possibly worn by warriors who had adopted the animal as their totem, thus invoking the protection of Epona, the horse goddess. Lime washing had a practical side as well, since the process coarsened and stiffened the hair, providing a degree of protection from blows to the head. The disadvantage was that repeated application caused burning to the scalp and the hair to fall out. It was also difficult to wear a helmet with lime-washed hair, although it is perhaps unlikely that the warrior would have desired or felt the need to do so, believing himself to be adequately protected by his totem. Warriors in Britain presented an even stranger spectacle due to their habit of painting or tattooing their bodies with woad, a plant from which a deep-blue dye was extracted. Similar customs exist in many ancient cultures, and as well as indicating social rank they almost invariably have a ritual significance. It is possible that the individual warrior believed himself to be protected and his strength enhanced by the sacred symbolism of the swirling forms on his face, arms and torso.

Chariot mount,
perhaps representing
a guardian deity,
1st century BC. (Lennart
Larsen, The National
Museum of Denmark)

OPPOSITE Detail of the
'Warrior' panel of the
Gundestrup cauldron
showing the carnyx, the
Celtic war horn. (akg-
images / Erich Lessing)

Both on and off the field of battle the Celtic warrior
sought to demonstrate his wealth and status by the quality
of his dress and equipment. Diodorus Siculus had this to say
about the way they dressed:

> The clothing they wear is striking: tunics and breeches dyed and
> embroidered in various colours. They also wear striped cloaks
> fastened with a brooch on the shoulder, heavy for winter and
> light for summer, in which are set checks, close together and
> of various hues. (*Historical Library*)

From contemporary descriptions such as this
and from the fragments of textiles recovered
from graves, a fair idea may be gained of the
clothes worn by the Celts. Most items were
colourful and well made of wool or linen.
Clothing worn by the nobility could be
embroidered with gold thread, and was sometimes
even made from silk. The reference to variegated
checks brings to mind the tweed or tartan-like
designs of a later age. Colours, however bright when
new, would fade quickly because of the vegetable dyes
used. The Celtic love of display and ornament was emphasized
by the jewellery they wore: 'They amass a great quantity of gold
which is used for ornament not only by the women but also by the men.
They wear bracelets on their wrists and arms, and heavy necklaces of solid gold, rings
of great value and even corselets.' (Diodorus Siculus, *Historical Library*)

Of all Celtic jewellery, the most impressive in the eyes of Mediterranean
commentators was the neck ring or torc. To the Romans it characterized the Celts
although it was not unique to them. The torc could be of gold, bronze or iron
according to the wealth of the wearer. It is quite possible that it possessed a symbolic
significance, since not all were made of precious metal. It was almost certainly an
indication of rank (the Gauls presented a golden torc to the Emperor Augustus that
was supposedly 45kg [99lb] in weight), with perhaps in some cases ritual or
religious overtones. From the 2nd century BC, torcs began to replace weapons in
elite burials, indicating a change in emphasis on the trappings of status in parallel
with the evolution of a Celtic urban society.

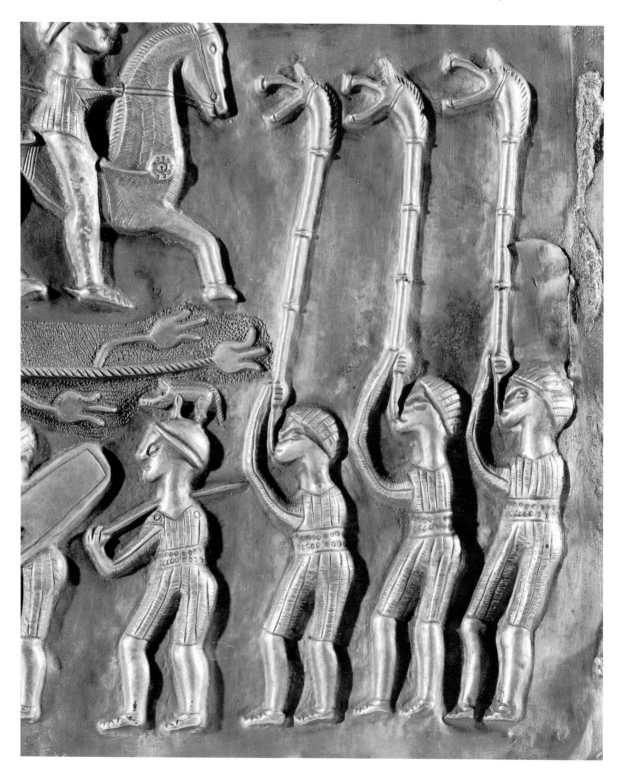

The great torc found at Snettisham, Norfolk, is made from an alloy of gold, silver and copper, and weighs just over 1kg. It has been dated to the mid-1st century BC. (Werner Forman Archive / British Museum, London)

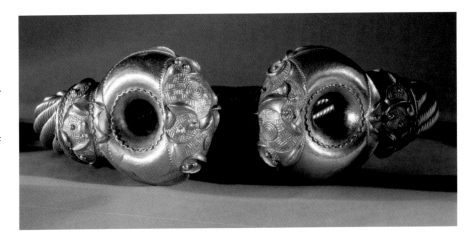

Archaeological finds also provide clues to the appearance of the Celtic military aristocracy. Male dress from the second half of the 5th century BC – tunic, cloak, close-fitting breeches and shoes with turned-up points – is depicted on brooches of this date found in central Europe. An engraved sword scabbard discovered in the cemetery at Halstatt in Austria, dating from the early La Tène period, portrays a line of infantrymen armed with spears and oval shields, followed by cavalry in helmets and a type of cuirass, armed with lances. Only one, perhaps their leader, carries a sword. They seem to be wearing shoes with pointed, turned-up toes similar to those found in the tomb of the so-called Hochdorf Prince. One of the plates of the Gundestrup cauldron (see p.98) represents a column of warriors on foot and on horseback whose appearance resembles that of the warriors on the Halstatt scabbard. They differ by their helmet crests: a bird, a wild boar, a pair of horns and a sun-wheel. The horses are now saddled, with a scabbard, and harnessed with embossed bronze or iron discs known as *phalerae* similar to those found in northern Italy and dated, like the Gundestrup cauldron itself, to the 1st century BC. The mounted warriors are still clad in close-fitting breeches and a type of jacket, possibly some kind of cuirass made of leather or metal plates, but are now equipped with spurs. The line of warriors on foot wear short breeches and tight jackets fastened at the waist by wide belts. The first six carry long oval shields with circular bosses and long spears; they are followed by a leader figure wearing a boar-crested helmet. Behind him stand three musicians blowing the famous Celtic war horn, the *carnyx* (see p.113).

This image of the Celtic warrior is very different from the horde of half-naked warriors usually presented in the accounts of classical authors and is equally far removed from the more modern popular perception of the barbarian or 'noble savage' that dates from the 19th century. It does, however, have significant parallels with representations of Etruscan military equipment of the 6th and 5th centuries BC. Stone statues from Glauberg and La Roquepertuse clearly show that similar equipment was adopted by the military elite of the transalpine Celts. The warriors who led the Celtic migrations into Italy and the armies that later invaded the Balkans were very likely dressed and equipped in this manner.

ARMS AND ARMOUR

The bearing of arms was the right and duty of every free man in Celtic society. It served to differentiate him, immediately and clearly, from the unfree majority. The basic equipment of the Celtic warrior was spear and shield. To this could be added a sword, a helmet and a mailshirt. Diodorus Siculus provides a detailed description of the Celtic warrior's arms and armour:

> Their arms include man-sized shields decorated according to individual taste. Some of these have projecting figures in bronze skilfully made not only for decoration but also for protection. They wear bronze helmets with large figures which give the wearer the appearance of enormous size. In some cases horns are attached, in others the foreparts of birds or beasts. Some of them have iron breastplates or chain mail while others fight naked. They carry long swords held by a chain of bronze or iron hanging on their right side. They brandish spears which have iron heads a cubit or more in length and a little less than two palms in breadth. Some are forged straight, others are twisted so that the blow does not merely cut the flesh but in withdrawing will lacerate the wound. (*Historical Library*)

Iron sword blade and spearheads from the Marne region of northern France, mid-5th century BC. (akg-images / Pietro Baguzzi)

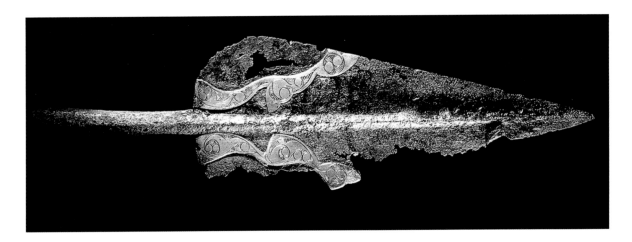

Iron spearhead with bronze appliqué recovered from the Thames, 1st century BC. Like the Battersea shield and Waterloo helmet, it was probably used not in battle but for display and as a gift to the gods. (Werner Forman Archive / The British Museum, London)

The Greek writer Strabo commented that the Celtic warrior carried two types of spear: a larger, heavier one for thrusting, and a smaller, lighter javelin that could be both thrown and used at close quarters. Spearheads of different shape, size and weight found at La Tène indicate a variety of uses. Ash was a common wood for the shaft, which was fitted with a bronze butt spike to provide a counterweight for the head. In Irish tales, spearshafts are described as having bands from head to foot, perhaps also of bronze. Two complete spears were recovered from the lake deposits at La Tène, each 2.5m (8ft 2in) long. Among the Hispanic Celts a spear made entirely of iron, called a *soliferrum*, was also used. Of varying length up to a maximum of 2m (6ft 6in), it was particularly effective at short range due to its barbed head, which gave it great penetration ability, much like the Roman *pilum*.

It seems likely that the spear was the mark of the warrior in the earlier Halstatt period. However, with the rise of the La Tène aristocracies, the sword came to symbolize the high-status warrior. The spread of La Tène culture in central and western Europe, and of Celtic mercenaries throughout the Mediterranean, can be traced by finds of the characteristic Celtic sword in male graves. Many of these weapons were elaborately decorated with precious metals and stones. The reconstruction of the Kirkburn sword and scabbard from Britain has shown that the original was made from over 70 pieces of iron, bronze and copper, and was inlaid with enamel and glass. As in other ancient cultures, blades were incised with symbolic forms that imbued the weapon with supernatural power. Sword blades found at La Tène measure about 60cm (23⅔in) in length. With improvements in ironworking techniques and the evolution of fighting styles as a result of direct contact with the Mediterranean world, as well as the increasing role of cavalry, longer blades became more common in the last two centuries BC. Celtic swords were worn on the right, suspended from a bronze or iron chain around the waist. The chain passed through a loop at the back of the scabbard and kept the weapon upright, helping to prevent the sword from becoming entangled with the warrior's legs as he walked or ran. Archaeological evidence has proved that Celtic swords were of high quality, flexible and with a sharp, strong cutting edge, contradicting Polybius' comments that in battle the blade quickly became so bent that the warrior had to straighten it with his foot. Confusion probably arose over the practice of ritually 'killing' a sword by deliberately bending it as part of a burial ceremony or sacrifice to the gods (see p.95). The quality and efficiency of the Celtic sword is made clear by Dionysius of Halicarnassus who described how the warrior would raise his sword above his head to deliver a downward stroke with his whole weight behind it. Together with the weight of the weapon itself, such a blow was capable of cutting through shield, armour and bone. When the legendary Cúchulainn faced the champion Edarcomhol, 'he struck him on the top of his head and split him to the navel'. (Kinsela, *Táin Bó Cuailnge*)

In Iberia, shorter swords predominated, although examples of La Tène styles have been discovered. The quality of the weapon is once again confirmed by the Roman adoption of the straight-bladed swords used by Hispanic mercenaries in the Punic Wars. The *gladius hispaniensis*, as it became known, remained the standard side arm of the Roman legionary for nearly 500 years. A curved-bladed sword, called a *falcata*, was the weapon that most characterized Iberians and Hispanic Celts alike, however. This was a single-edge slashing weapon about 60cm (23⅗in) long of such quality that, according to Diodorus Siculus, no helmet, shield or bone could resist its stroke. Unlike the long-bladed La Tène swords, the falcata was slung on the left hip by a baldric, which enabled it to be carried almost horizontally in its scabbard. Its resemblance to the Greek *machaira* or *kopis* has led archaeologists to suggest that it was copied from examples brought to Iberia by Greek migrants and traders or by mercenaries in Greek pay around the 6th century BC. Another possible explanation is that it evolved from a curved knife dating back to the Halstatt period and which spread from central Europe to Greece and Italy as well as Iberia.

It is not clear to what extent the bow and sling were used in Celtic warfare. There is little archaeological evidence for the former, although some iron arrowheads have been discovered at the site of Alésia in Gaul. However, there is a great deal of evidence for the latter in the form of the vast stockpiles of sling stones that have been unearthed within several of the hillforts in southern Britain, most notably at Maiden Castle in Dorset, an indication that their use was a major factor in the defence of these sites. It has been suggested that the elaborate arrangement of

The Kirkburn sword, found in east Yorkshire, is a marvel of the Celtic metalworker's art. It was made from over 70 pieces of iron, bronze and copper, and was inlaid with enamel and glass. Dated to the 1st century BC. (© Trustees of the British Museum / 1987,0404.2)

Iron sword found in the territory of the Aedui, near Chalon-sur-Saône, 1st century BC. (bpk / Museum für Vor-und Frühgeschichte, Staatliche Museen zu Berlin, photo Claudia Pump)

OPPOSITE The magnificent Battersea shield recovered from the Thames is made of sheet bronze and was far too fragile to be used in war. A masterpiece of the Celtic metalworker's art, it was probably a ceremonial item created for display or as a votive offering. The panels are inlaid with red glass. (Werner Forman Archive / British Museum, London)

the ramparts at the entrances to the hillforts was specifically designed to maximize the effectiveness of this particular weapon. Nevertheless, the use of the sling is not mentioned in any account of a set-piece battle. An explanation can perhaps be found by recalling the ethos of the warrior. Both the bow and the sling are missile weapons, best employed at a distance from the enemy. Arrows and sling stones can be directed towards an enemy in large volleys or showers, but they will not all find a target. They do not even have to be particularly accurate to be effective or dissuasive. The Gallic leader Vercingetorix is reported to have called for all the archers who could be found in Gaul to be sent to him to make up for his losses after the siege of Avaricum. The implication here would seem to be that, despite the many thousands of warriors who were already fighting with him (according to Caesar, over 250,000 were present at Alésia), these archers were not among them and might not otherwise have been expected to fight. Furthermore, the principal engagements following Avaricum were two other sieges, one at Gergovia and the final defeat of the Gauls at Alésia. Vercingetorix apparently used his archers to defend his strongholds just as slingers defended British hillforts. Perhaps the Celtic warrior used neither bow nor sling because they were not considered to be a warrior's weapons. His goal on the battlefield was to engage the enemy at close quarters with spear and sword, and to measure his prowess against that of his opponent. To stand off and shoot at him from a distance would therefore be considered dishonourable.

The warrior's principal protection was his shield. Celtic shields were generally oval in shape or sometimes an elongated hexagon. They were made of thin planks of oak or lime wood covered in leather. The resulting construction was both light and resilient, essential to the warrior who held the shield by a central horizontal handgrip, wielding it not only to defend himself but also offensively to punch at his opponent. His hand was protected by a hollow wooden boss that sometimes extended into a central spine to reinforce the face of the shield. The boss was often itself reinforced by a bronze or iron plate. More rarely, the shield might be edged with a metal strip to better deflect blows. Examples discovered at La Tène measure approximately 1.1m (3ft 7in) by 0.6m (1ft 11in). Later evidence from Gaul in the 1st century BC suggests an increase in size to 1.3m (4ft 3in) or 1.4m (4ft 7in) in length, perhaps influenced by the large body shields used by the Romans. A smaller shield, known as the *caetra* by the Romans, was also used by the Hispanic Celts.

Between 30 and 60cm (11¾in and 23½in) in diameter, it was reinforced by a large metal boss and other fittings on the face. Particularly favoured by the Lusitani, its use with the falcata made a formidable combination in single combat.

Diodorus Siculus wrote that Celtic shields were decorated according to individual taste, though there is little archaeological evidence as to what form this might have taken. A possible indication is given by the bronze outline figure of a boar that was riveted to the Witham shield recovered from the river of the same name in Lincolnshire. It is likely that the Celtic warrior embellished his shield in a similar, albeit simpler way, with stylized representations of his personal totem or guardian spirit, or perhaps more general Otherworld symbols, such as the sun-wheel, in order to invoke their protective power. Some shields, like that found at Witham, were faced with sheet bronze; others, like the magnificent example found in the river Thames at Battersea, were made entirely of bronze. They were far too fragile to be used in war and were almost certainly ceremonial items created especially for display and as gifts to the gods.

Apart from the shield, protection on the battlefield was enhanced by body armour in the form of a helmet and mailshirt. These would be more usual among the nobility and other high-status warriors. In the Halstatt and early La Tène periods, helmets were made of bronze. Iron helmets first appeared in the 4th century BC and gradually replaced the softer alloy, possibly in response to the development of the long slashing sword. There would have been some sort of padding on the inside to

Bronze helmet found in the Thames, with characteristic wide neckguard. Possibly inspired by the 'Coolus' type of helmet used by the Romans. (Werner Forman Archive / British Museum, London)

protect the skull, and holes in the rim indicate the presence of fastening straps. They usually had a neckguard and often hinged cheek pieces as an additional protection for the face, a feature that may have been adopted from Etruscan models. A fitting on the crown of the helmet enabled a plume or crest to be attached. As suggested by the Gundestrup cauldron, the crest could take the form of animals or birds with special symbolic significance. Perhaps the most striking example is the Çiumesti helmet from Romania (see p.49), found complete with its elaborate raven crest and articulated wings. This and many others were intended more for display than for battle. The horned Waterloo helmet (see pp.142–3) dredged up from the Thames mud, and the fabulous Agris helmet (see p.81), discovered in fragments in western France, which was made from iron but plated with gold and decorated with bronze, silver and coral, are but two examples. By the mid-1st century BC, a newer style of helmet had evolved in Gaul, typified by the so-called Agen helmet unearthed at the site of Alésia. This type is sometimes referred to as the 'battle bowler'. It was adopted by the Romans after Caesar's campaigns and became the principal model for the legionary helmet for the next three centuries.

From the evidence we possess, it is clear that armour was worn by the Celts from an early period. The mounted warriors depicted on the Halstatt scabbard appear to be wearing a kind of padded tunic with a skirt of leather straps, known as *pteruges* in Greek, to protect the lower body. The statues excavated from the Glauberg elite burials near Frankfurt-am-Main in southern Germany, which have been dated to the late 6th century BC, are clad in armour that is reminiscent of the padded linen cuirasses worn by Greek and Etruscan hoplites at this time, complete with the characteristic shoulder pieces that are tied down at the front. Similar cuirasses also appear on the seated warrior statues discovered at the Entremont oppidum in the south of France.

At some point after 400 BC, Celtic metalworkers mastered the necessary techniques to develop their own unique form of body armour. Mail, sometimes called chain mail or ring mail, consists of small metal rings linked together to form a close-knit mesh. Although it can be punctured by a spear or shorn by the blow from an axe or sword, when worn over a leather undershirt it provides a considerable measure of protection against wounds that might otherwise be incapacitating or fatal, while its flexibility does not impair movement. Originally, mail would have been reserved for noble warriors, since its fabrication was a lengthy process. Surviving fragments have revealed two different methods: rings punched out from a disc and rings cut from a wire twisted around a wooden dowl to form a spiral. The latter were then riveted shut, to reduce the chance of their splitting open when subjected

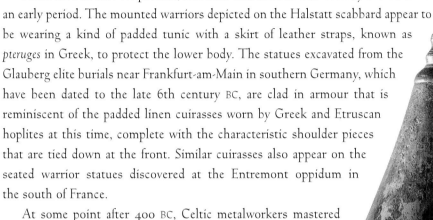

Bronze, gold-plated helmet from the Marne area of northern France. A horsehair plume would have fitted into the top. Dated to the 3rd century BC. (akg-images / Erich Lessing)

The Witham shield is interesting not only because of its ceremonial character but also because of its offset boss and the very faint outline of a stylized boar, which was originally riveted to the bronze face of the shield. (Werner Forman Archive / British Museum, London)

to a thrusting attack or a hit by an arrow. Remnants of iron mail appear for the first time in graves dating from the 3rd century BC. Early examples seem to have been reinforced with shoulder pieces like the hoplite cuirass, and on occasions by a mantle that protected the entire upper back and chest. It is interesting to note the comment by the Greek author Pausanias that the only defensive armour of the Galatoi was their shields. Does this imply that mail was not worn by Galatian nobles at the time of the Celtic invasion of the Balkans? It was certainly being used to great effect by the Celts in northern Italy, so much so that the Romans again adopted the technology of their traditional enemies for their own troops.

HEROIC NUDITY

Greeks and Romans were disconcerted on occasions to be faced with numbers of Celtic warriors who fought completely naked. There are several references to this practice up to the 2nd century BC, the most notable being the account of the battle of Telamon, in which Polybius claimed that the Celts discarded their clothes because they would be a hindrance in the thorny, scrub-covered terrain. Other accounts mention naked Celtic warriors at the battle of Cannae in 216 BC and in battles against the Galatians a century later. Apart from a practical aspect – pieces of dirty cloth forced into a wound are difficult to extract and will lead to infection – nudity on the battlefield almost certainly had some religious or ritual significance. Polybius noted the 'proud confidence' of the Gaesatae at Telamon. Protected and empowered by the divine forces to whom he had dedicated himself, the warrior felt no need for either armour or clothing. The fact that he carried a shield did not contradict the assumption of divine protection. Like the spear and sword, the shield was part of the warrior's panoply; it was not only his right but also his duty to bear it.

THE FACE OF BATTLE

Polybius' vivid account of the battle of Telamon shows that a Celtic host drawn up for battle presented an impressive and daunting sight. It also reveals that the deployment of a Celtic army on the field of battle was no mere 'column of mob'. Deployment would probably have been by tribal contingents. Within these contingents, clans would deploy as separate bodies, perhaps according to an acknowledged or traditional pecking order. The nobles

Seated figure of a noble or a deity from the Celto-Ligurian sanctuary at La Roquepertuse, southern France, 3rd to 2nd century BC. Note the indication of Greek- or Etruscan-style stiffened linen armour on the upper body. (The Art Archive / Musée d'Archéologie méditerranéenne, Marseille / Dagli Orti)

and other high-status warriors would stand in the front line accompanied by their retinues. To identify each grouping in the battle line and to act as rallying points, the guardian deities of tribe and clan were carried into battle as standards topped with carved or cast figures of their animal forms. Just like the eagles of Rome, these were sacred symbols. Caesar describes the Gauls taking solemn vows before them prior to setting off to war.

Bronze warrior figurine from northern Gaul, 1st century BC. (akg-images / Erich Lessing)

As the Celtic host deployed for battle and caught sight of the enemy they set up a dreadful din. Each warrior gave full voice to his war cry or battle chant, doubtless mingled with taunts, insults and obscenities aimed at his opponent. Describing the battle of Allia just before the sack of Rome, Livy wrote of the Gauls, 'They are given to wild outbursts and fill the air with hideous songs and varied cries.' And of the Galatians of Asia Minor, 'Their songs as they go into battle, their yells and leaping, and the dreadful noise of arms as they beat their shields in some ancestral custom – all this is done with one purpose: to terrify their enemies.' (*History of Rome*)

To the cacophony of the warriors themselves was added the sound of the carnyx, the Celtic war horn. The carnyx was a long horn with a head and mouth in the form of an animal, often that of a wild boar. A particularly fine example in bronze was discovered at Deskford in Scotland in the early 19th century. It has been dated to the mid-1st century BC and is comparable with those featured on the Gundestrup cauldron (see p.113). When first excavated, the Deskford carnyx was found to have a wooden tongue or clapper in the mouth, which probably increased the vibration of the harsh braying sound.

As the opposing armies faced each other, prominent warriors would step forward and issue a challenge:

> When the armies are drawn up they are wont to advance in front of the line of battle and challenge the bravest of their opponents to single combat. When someone accepts the challenge, they recite the heroic deeds of their ancestors and proclaim their own valour, at the same time abusing and belittling their opponent in an attempt to rob him of his fighting spirit.
>
> (Diodorus Siculus, *Historical Library*)

Livy wrote of an incident when a Celtic warrior goaded a Roman into accepting his challenge by the simple expedient of poking his tongue out and laughing at him. The Roman had the last laugh, however, and killed his tormentor. On the point of robbing an enemy of his fighting spirit, in a similar confrontation the extent of the warrior's faith in the power and favour of the gods is revealed by the utter collapse of the Celt's morale when a raven appeared to land on the Roman's helmet before flying threateningly towards the warrior. The will of the gods of battle had been clearly demonstrated; further resistance was useless and he was promptly dispatched. In Irish myth, Badbh, the goddess of battle, and Morrigan, the Queen of Darkness, both manifested themselves as a crow. The *Táin* tells of the death of Cúchulainn when both deities perched on his shoulder in the midst of battle, encouraging the men of Connacht to strike him down and take his head.

Bronze spearheads from Gaul, 4th century BC. (Musée des Antiquités nationales, St Germain-en-Laye, France / Bridgeman Art Library)

Single combat was one of the most effective ways for a warrior to gain or enhance his prestige. In offering a challenge on the battlefield he fulfilled the boasts made at the feast, confirming his honour, and at the same time calling into question that of his opponents. It was an integral part of the Celtic way of war that enabled the greatest and most ambitious warriors to play their own individual part in the ritual of battle. Their courage would be remembered in the songs of the bards together with the heroes of Celtic myth and legend. Single combat also served to increase tension among the other warriors who were working themselves into a fury with war cries and the clashing of weapons on shields. It has been suggested that the ritual of single combat was originally a way of limiting conflicts between early Celtic communities which, while being an integral part of the social structure, was hedged around with conventions and taboos. Through single combat, the whole clan or tribe could participate in battle. Following a series of combats between champions, the issue would be clearly decided and accepted by the onlookers who would then disperse. While the conduct of the warrior was indeed governed by strict rules, to assume that the companions of the one who had just been killed and beheaded would meekly retire from the field, any more than the followers of the victor would stand by and watch them go when both were at a peak of frenzy, is to disregard many accounts of the Celts in battle and also the psyche of the warrior himself. The *Táin* contains a graphic description of the battle frenzy of the hero Cúchulainn:

Then the madness of battle came upon him. You would have thought that every hair was being driven into his head, that every hair was tipped with a spark of fire. He closed one eye until it was no wider than the eye of a needle; he opened the other until it was as big as a wooden bowl. He bared his teeth from jaw to ear and opened his mouth until the gullet could be seen. (Kinsela, *Táin Bó Cuailnge*)

The wild charge of the Celtic warrior was the inevitable consequence of his battle madness. Its ferocity was legendary and rightly feared throughout the classical Mediterranean world. However, if those facing the charge were sufficiently prepared, protected and above all disciplined, then there was a good chance that the force of the attack could be blunted. Once this happened, the Celts' psychology of war worked against them. Celtic armies were fragile and unstable by nature, made up of masses of individuals all competing with one another for status and glory. If their initial charge failed to break the enemy line, the Celts would tend to become discouraged. Their battle frenzy would begin to ebb, the initiative would pass to the defenders, and they would almost certainly lose the battle. Despite the well attested

The Amfreville helmet, discovered in a river in northern France. Bronze, decorated with iron, gold and red enamel. Dated to the 4th century BC. (akg-images / Erich Lessing)

occasions when Celtic armies fought stubbornly to the death, their lack of staying power in the face of more disciplined armies gave rise to their reputation for fickleness among the Romans, whose concept of battle was very different. Both sides considered that the other did not 'fight by the rules'.

Caesar wrote of the Nervii at the battle of the Sambre during the Gallic War:

> They suddenly dashed out in full force and swooped down on our cavalry which they easily routed. Then they ran down to the river at such an incredible speed that almost at the same moment they seemed to be at the edge of the forest, in the water and already upon us. (*The Conquest of Gaul*)

However, despite the mad rush of the warrior and his desire to close with his opponent, Tacitus said in his account of the battle of Mons Graupius that 'The fighting began with an exchange of missiles. The Britons showed both steadiness and skill in parrying our spears with their huge swords or catching them on their small shields, while they themselves rained volleys on us.' (*Agricola*)

Having hurled his javelins at close range, the warrior battered his way into the enemy's ranks, punching with his shield, thrusting with his spear or slashing with his sword. Against other Celts the battle was quickly transformed into a series of individual combats. The chaos and almost unimaginable bloodletting was portrayed by an unknown Irish author in the 9th century AD:

> Then the two armies made for each other. Fierce was the onslaught they made on either side. Bitter sights were seen there: the white fog of chalk and lime from the shields as they were struck by the edges of the swords and the points of the spears, which were skilfully parried by the heroes; the beating and shattering of the shield-bosses as they were belaboured with swords and stones; the noise of the pelting weapons; the gushing and shedding of blood and gore from the limbs of the champions and the sides of the warriors. (Jackson, *A Celtic Miscellany*)

Against the disciplined, close-order units of the armies of Greece and Rome, such tactics were less successful. Breakthroughs were difficult to achieve since neither cohort nor phalanx would obligingly disperse to allow the Celts to engage in single combat. Caesar's reference to the Gauls fighting in dense masses can be understood in these terms, as they became stacked up against the Roman shield wall, the majority of them unable to come to grips with the defenders. In his account of the battle of Mons Graupius, Tacitus noted the disorder and panic among the Britons once their initial attack had failed. Nevertheless, we have several accounts of the determination of the Celtic warrior to carry on the fight to the death rather than run from the field. Caesar wrote of the Nervii:

> But the enemy, even in their desperate plight, showed such bravery that when their front ranks had fallen those immediately behind stood on their prostrate bodies to fight; and when these too fell and the corpses were piled high, the survivors still kept hurling javelins as though from the top of a mound, and flung back the spears they caught on their shield.
> (*The Conquest of Gaul*)

The convictions that led the warrior to fight on and, seemingly, to embrace death are difficult for us to understand and appreciate. In the end it comes back to a question of personal honour explicable in part by the close ties between patron and client, and the obsessive desire of the warrior to gain prestige and stand well with his fellows, and perhaps also with his foes.

British coin from the 1st century AD depicting a Celtic cavalryman. Note the classical-style helmet. (Werner Forman Archive / British Museum, London)

FIRST KNIGHT

Tacitus wrote that the main strength of the Celts lay in their infantry. While this remained the case throughout the Celtic world in the La Tène period, there is, nevertheless, a great deal of evidence that they were also accomplished horsemen. Elite graves dating back to the 8th century BC are characterized by horse gear and wagons, emphasizing the importance of the horse as a status symbol for the Halstatt chieftains and implying the growing role of cavalry in war, possibly under the influence of the nomadic Scythians. Cavalry figures feature prominently on both the Halstatt scabbard and the Gundestrup cauldron and may give us an idea of their appearance.

The Celts revered the horse for its courage, speed and sexual vigour. The animal was a symbol of the sun god, who was often portrayed as a horseman bearing a thunderbolt as a spear and the solar wheel as a shield. In Welsh myth, the hero Culwych appeared in this manner at Arthur's court. The Irish horse goddess Macha was also a goddess of war. Her name appears in a reference by Pausanias to the Galatians' cavalry tactic called the *trimarcisia*:

Horse harness decoration
made of bronze with
enamel inlay, from Britain,
late 1st century BC. (akg-
images / Erich Lessing)

Horse harness decoration made of bronze with enamel inlay, from Britain, late 1st century BC. (akg-images / Erich Lessing)

To each horsemen were attached two attendants who were themselves skilled riders. When the Galatian horsemen were engaged, these attendants remained behind the ranks. If the horseman were killed, one of the attendants would replace him; if injured, the second would help him back to camp. Should his horse be hurt, one of the attendants would bring him a remount. (*Description of Greece*)

An indication of the effectiveness of this tactic is given by Caesar, who wrote of the Celtic cavalry he encountered in Britain:

A further difficulty was that they never fought in close order, but in a very open formation, and had reserves posted here and there; in this way the various groups covered one another's retreat, and fresh troops replaced those that were tired. (*The Conquest of Gaul*)

A century before the Celts invaded Greece they had fought as mercenaries in Greek armies, where their skill as horsemen had been particularly valued. Xenophon, a Greek chronicler and military commander during the Peloponnesian War (431–404 BC), described their use of the 'feigned flight' tactic against the Thebans:

They charged towards the Thebans, threw their javelins, and then dashed away as the enemy moved towards them, often turning to throw more javelins. While pursuing these tactics, they sometimes dismounted. If they were attacked, they would easily leap onto their horses and retreat. Then, if the enemy pursued them, they would suddenly turn and shower them with more missiles. In this way, they manipulated the entire Theban army, compelling them to advance or fall back at will. (*Hellenica*)

Pausanias also mentioned the Galatoi riding onto the battlefield and then dismounting to engage the enemy, tethering their mounts by means of small pegs attached to the reins that they pushed in to the ground. Such examples suggest that, at this period, mounted Celtic warriors engaged in battle that was more reminiscent of the heroic single combat than of the mass brawl of the warrior on foot.

Celtic mercenary horsemen, especially from Iberia and Gaul, were much sought after by the Mediterranean powers, fighting for Hannibal in the Second Punic War (218–202 BC) and later on behalf of Rome, when they provided Caesar with much of his mounted arm. At the battle of Raphia in 217 BC, a force of 4,000 Celtic horsemen fought with the Egyptian army of Ptolemy IV against the Seleucid king of Syria, Antiochus III. Their attack on the disorganized Syrian pike phalanx was a contributing factor in the defeat of Antiochus. In the late 1st century BC, 400 Celtic cavalry formed part of the bodyguard of King Herod the Great. They had previously served Queen Cleopatra of Egypt in a similar capacity and were presented to Herod as a gift by Octavian, the future Emperor Augustus.

The growing emphasis on cavalry among the Celts themselves from the end of the 3rd century BC onwards can be seen in the increased length of sword blades, some reaching almost 90cm (35½in) in length. Such swords would be too long to be easily wielded by a warrior on foot. Coins struck in the 1st century BC by the Boii in Pannonia show cavalrymen charging with long swords. The introduction of the four-pommel saddle may explain this development in part. This type of

The bronze Chertsey shield, another rich item recovered from a river in Britain and destined as a gift to the gods rather than for use in war. (© Trustees of the British Museum / PS232422)

saddle, which is thought to have originated among the nomadic tribes of the Asiatic steppe, from where it spread to central and western Europe in the latter half of the 1st millennium BC, provided the rider with a seat that was as secure as if he were using stirrups, which were not invented for almost another thousand years. Spurs were used, however. Improvements in stock breeding were also a factor. There is convincing archaeological evidence of improvements in the breeding of horses in the last two centuries BC, especially in central Gaul. Significantly, there is little evidence of this in Britain, where high-status warriors fought from chariots in conjunction with light cavalry using similar tactics to those described by Pausanias and Xenophon above.

The change in emphasis from skirmishing with javelins to shock tactics using a spear and long sword can be detected in Caesar's description of the cavalry engagements during his campaigns in Gaul. By this period, the elite Gallic warriors who provided the urban aristocracies with their armed retainers were almost entirely cavalry, armed with spear and long slashing sword, protected by an iron helmet and mailshirt, and mounted on a larger horse capable of bearing the weight of the rider and his equipment. To the Romans, they were the equivalent of their own 'knightly' class, the *equites*. Interestingly, this image of the armoured Celtic 'knight' brings to mind the heavy cavalry of the early mediaeval period, the so-called 'Dark Ages', who were equipped with mailshirt and iron helmet, and who fought with spear and long sword. It is tempting to suggest that the origins of the knights that dominated the battlefields of the Middle Ages, especially in France, can perhaps be traced in part to the Celtic cavalryman of the later Iron Age.

The Gallic horsemen who accompanied the Roman army of Crassus during the invasion of Parthia in 53 BC would probably have been equipped like this. At the disastrous battle of Carrhae, the Celts themselves fell victim to the feigned flight tactics of the Parthian horse archers. Their frustration and reaction is reminiscent of the Gaesatae at the battle of Telamon. The Greek author Plutarch described the scene:

Crassus saw that his rear was about to be attacked. He ordered his son, Publius, to take 1,300 Gallic horsemen, 500 archers and eight cohorts, to attack the Parthian horse archers. The Parthians galloped away with this Roman force in pursuit. Once Publius was far enough away from the Roman main body, the horse archers wheeled about and were joined by a larger number of Parthians including the cataphracts. Publius led the Gauls against the cataphracts. Because their spears could not penetrate the cataphracts' armour, the frenzied Gauls seized the enemy's lances, pulling them to the ground. They also leapt beneath the Parthian horses to attack their exposed bellies, and even drove their own horses onto the lances. (*Lives*)

CHARIOTS OF THE GODS

Archaeological evidence suggests that the Celtic chariot was a specialized version of the two- and four-wheeled vehicles used in funerary rites in the early Iron Age. The burial of two-wheeled chariots in elite graves from Champagne to Bohemia is one of the principal elements that characterize the development of the La Tène culture in the mid-5th century BC. This practice was probably adopted from the Celts of the Golasecean culture, where it occurs in warrior graves from the end of the

Embossed silver *phalera* from Italy, 1st century BC. Such discs often portrayed a circle of human heads. Note the triple 'S' in the centre. (The Art Archive / Museo Civico Romana, Brescia / Dagli Orti)

7th century BC, although in Britain chariots were almost certainly used in war as far back as the middle Bronze Age, in the 2nd millennium BC. The chariot was a parade vehicle that emphasized the high status of the warrior who rode in it, but which was also intended for use in battle both as a means of transport and as a fighting platform. Diodorus Siculus wrote that the Gauls used two-horse chariots for journeys and in battle, which carried a chieftain and a charioteer.

The Celtic chariot consisted of a platform about 1m (3ft 3in) square, carried on an axle and a pair of spoked, iron-rimmed wheels approximately 0.9m (2ft 11in) in diameter, and harnessed via a pole and a yoke to two ponies. The sides of the vehicle were double loops of bent wood. From depictions on coins, it seems likely that at least part of the sides was filled and decorated with wicker or leather panels. The front and rear were left open for ease of access. The floor was possibly also of leather, providing a simple form of suspension. A more recent theory suggests that leather straps were attached to the loops on the sides of the chariot. These straps supported the platform independently from the outer framework which was fixed to the axle and pole. Tests conducted with a full-size reconstructed chariot have proved the feasibility of this method of construction. The elite symbolic nature of the vehicle was reflected in the quality of the fittings and the care taken in its construction. Metalwork was often inlaid with enamel, glass and coral; a surviving wheel from Scotland was found to be made from three different woods. Harnesses were also richly decorated.

Caesar was surprised to discover that the Britons were still using the chariot in war, a practice that had died out among the continental Celts almost two centuries before. He gave a detailed description of how they were employed on the battlefield:

> In chariot fighting the Britons begin by driving all over the field hurling javelins. Generally, the terror inspired by the horses and the noise of the wheels is sufficient to throw their opponent's ranks into disorder. Then, after making their way between the squadrons of their own cavalry, they jump down from the chariots and engage on foot. In the meantime, the charioteers retire a short distance from the battle and place their vehicles in such a position that their masters, if hard pressed by numbers, have an easy means of retreat to their own lines. Thus, they combine the mobility of cavalry with the staying power of infantry. (*The Conquest of Gaul*)

The chariots were particularly effective against patrols and foraging parties:

> When the Romans were busy foraging, scattered and with their weapons laid aside, the Britons suddenly attacked; they swarmed around with chariots and cavalry, killing a few and throwing the rest into confusion before they could form up.

There was a fierce engagement as the British cavalry and chariots clashed with our cavalry on the march. However, our men prevailed and drove the enemy into the woods and hills, killing a good many of them though suffering a number of casualties themselves through pushing the pursuit too far. Then, after a while, when our men were off their guard and fortifying the camp, the Britons suddenly rushed out of the woods, charged down on the outposts on picket duty and started a fierce battle there. (Caesar, *The Conquest of Gaul*)

These two passages provide a good illustration of the combined tactics used by the British horsemen and chariot warriors to harass and snipe at Roman forces feeling their way in unfamiliar territory. The use of cavalry and chariots together in a mutually supporting role suggests that the latter were still regarded as more becoming to the status of the noble warrior. The ambush and sudden charge from cover were favoured tactics of the Celts, and recall the ritual of the raid with its emphasis on surprise attack and skirmish. The reference to chariots driving about the battlefield recalls the intimidation of an opponent with noise and then the frenzied charge. Caesar wrote of the panic caused by chariots being driven at speed towards the Roman line. Similarly, a noble stepping down from the chariot to fight hand-to-hand after an exchange of missiles while the chariot withdraws ready to pick him up later recalls the *trimarcisia* tactics of the mounted warrior. The custom of single combat between nobles or heroes of equal status is also inferred. Overall, the use of chariots in battle by the Britons presents a style of combat of an earlier era, better suited to the low-intensity warfare between clans or tribes than to total war against the Romans. The ritual aspect of combat between chariot warriors is illustrated in a comment by the queen of Tara's

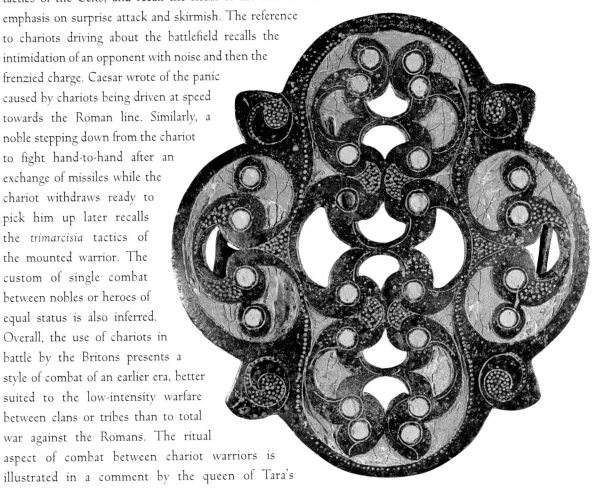

Bronze plaque with enamel decoration, probably part of a horse harness. Found in northern France, it is thought to be British in origin. Dated to the 1st or 2nd century BC. (Werner Forman Archive / Musée archéologique de Breteuil)

charioteer: 'Wait a minute until I turn the chariot around to the right with the sun, to draw down the power of the sign.' (Kinsela, *Táin Bó Cuailnge*) Turning the chariot to the right, or clockwise, in the same way that the sun appears to circle the earth, would therefore invoke the Otherworldly power. At the same time, the warrior presented his shielded side to his opponent. To do so in full sight of the enemy could only be construed one way. Cúchulainn's charioteer, Loegh, says in an Irish tale from the 9th century, '"Here is the chariot back again, and it has turned its left side towards us." "That is an insult that cannot be endured," replied Cúchulainn.' (Kinsela, *Táin Bó Cuailnge*)

The effectiveness of the chariot against troops unused to it was also due in no small measure to the skill of the charioteer, as Caesar wrote:

> By daily training and practice they attain such proficiency that even on a steep slope they are able to control the horses at full gallop, and to check and turn them in a moment. They can run along the chariot pole, stand on the yoke and get back into the chariot as quick as lightning. (*The Conquest of Gaul*)

Diodorus Siculus described charioteers as freemen, chosen by the nobles from among the ranks of the lower classes, and employed also as shield bearers. The relationship between the warrior and his charioteer was a particularly close one. The warrior effectively placed his life in the hands of his driver, whose skill and responsibility gave him his own particular status. The value placed on the charioteer is stressed in a 9th-century Irish manuscript that tells of a meeting between Cúchulainn and his enemy's charioteer. Despite his fearsome reputation, Cúchulainn reassures the other that he never kills charioteers. The charioteer, for all his skill, was chosen from a different social class. The *Táin* has an interesting reference to the special status of the charioteer: 'He placed the charioteer's sign on his brow ... a circle of deep yellow, shaped on an anvil's edge.' The cost of maintaining a chariot, horses and a charioteer, as well as the demands of the intensive training described by Caesar, indicate that the cavalry elite was recruited from the ranks of the nobility, the only class in Celtic society with the necessary time and means to devote to it.

AFTERMATH

From the accounts of Greek and Roman commentators, it is clear that the Celtic warrior had no fear of death in battle. It was an inseparable part of his life. A hero's death in war would ensure that his name and reputation would be remembered. The warrior's attitude to death is also illustrated by the vernacular literature of the later Celts and by archaeological evidence. As mentioned previously, the Celts lived in an environment where the worlds of the living and the dead were closely intertwined. The Otherworld was perceived as being very much like the world of mortal men, but without pain, disease or old age. However, for those who suffered the humiliation of being taken alive, a different fate could be expected.

Fragment of a stone sculpture of a head held by a hand, from the oppidum of Entremont. Dated to the 3rd to 2nd century BC. (akg-images / Erich Lessing)

THE SPOILS OF WAR

To the victor went the spoils of war. In addition to the heads of the vanquished, cattle, gold and women were especially prized as booty. Acquisition of wealth, and thereby status and prestige, was one of the principal motives that drove the Celtic warrior to wage war. The riches of the Mediterranean world were a major factor in the Celtic migrations of the 4th and 3rd centuries BC, and they continued to tempt groups of mercenaries. Polybius describes how, on the eve of the battle of Telamon, they had become victims of their own success:

> The commanders of the Gauls held a council of war. At this, Aneroestes argued that since they had captured so much booty (for the number of prisoners and cattle, and the quantities of plunder they had taken were enormous) they should not give battle again and put all their gains at risk, but should return home in safety. (*The Histories*)

Wise words on the part of Aneroestes. However, the amount of loot they had amassed slowed the Celtic army so much that it was caught by the Romans and destroyed.

Booty taken in war was not intended for the warrior's personal use, the exception being the head of an opponent killed in single combat. Enemies taken in war were dedicated to the gods, along with their arms and armour, and other precious objects:

> They vow to Mars the booty that they hope to take, and after a victory they sacrifice the captives, both animal and human, and collect the rest of the spoils in one spot. Among many of the tribes great piles can be seen on consecrated ground. It is almost unknown for anyone, in defiance of religious law, to conceal his booty at home or to remove anything placed there. Such a crime is punishable by a terrible death under torture. (Caesar, *The Conquest of Gaul*)

RITUAL SUICIDE

Although a fight to the death rather than a humiliating surrender was to be preferred, there were times when this was not possible. Rather than be taken alive, therefore, and suffer torture and death or be sold into slavery at the hands of his captors, the warrior would prefer to commit suicide. Polybius tells us of Aneroestes, one of the Celtic chieftains at Telamon, who 'fled from the battlefield with a few of his followers and found a refuge where he and the whole of his retinue took their own lives'. (*The Histories*)

Other examples are not lacking, including Brennus following the retreat of the Galatoi from Delphi, and, perhaps the best known of all, Boudica after the collapse

OPPOSITE
Stone heads from the oppidum of the Saluvii at Entremont. (akg-images / Erich Lessing)

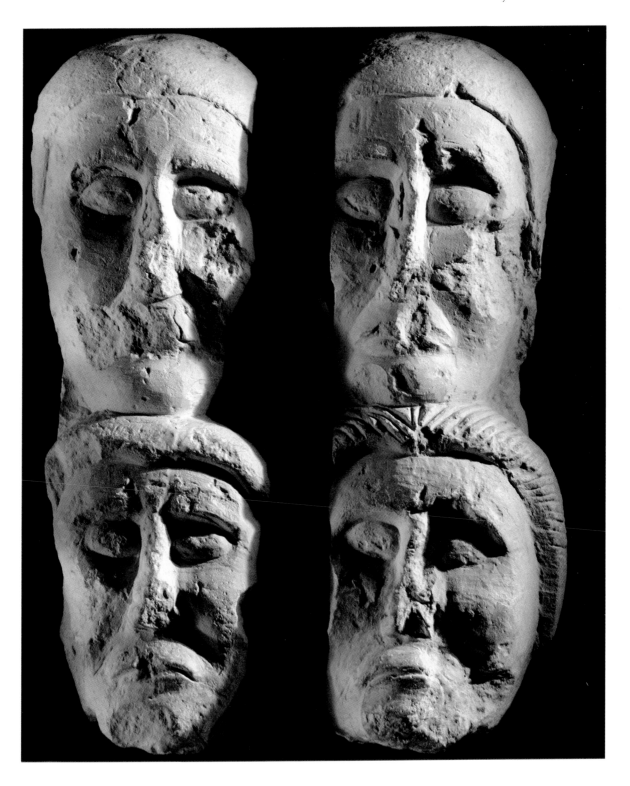

of the revolt of the Iceni. Caesar's reference to Catuvolcus of the Eburones, who committed suicide by hanging himself from an elm tree, hints strongly at the ritual nature of the act, a self-sacrifice in fact. The striking image that stood in the temple of Athena in Pergamon, which showed a warrior stabbing himself having just killed his wife, is a clear indication of the impact of the Celtic warrior's moral code of conduct on the Greek and Roman mind. Ever conscious of his personal standing and his obligations in this world, and his *geissi* sworn to the gods, for the Celtic warrior failure was simply not an option. To fail on the field of battle, where he sought to fulfil the boasts and pledges he had made at the feast and where his every action could be judged by his peers, was personally and socially unacceptable. Honour demanded that the highest price be paid.

SLAVERY

Increased contact with the Mediterranean and Celtic worlds produced a corresponding increase in the value of slaves as a trading commodity. It was a trend that contributed also to the growing intensity of warfare among the Celts themselves. The fate of the great majority of warriors taken in battle, therefore, was to be sold. They were too valuable to be sacrificed. As we have already noted, Diodorus Siculus remarked that a Celtic slave could be bought in exchange for an amphora of wine. The seller would share the traded wine among his followers to enhance his status. As the demand grew for wine and other Mediterranean prestige goods, so did the need to find more slaves to barter. Celt and Roman soon came to depend on one another. By the 1st century BC thousands of slaves were required every year to maintain the labour force in Italy. Not all came from Britain and Gaul, though Caesar's campaigns brought in vast numbers, on occasions whole populations. Some warriors found a kind of honourable death in the arena, but most ended their days in the fields toiling to produce the very wine they coveted so much.

OPPOSITE Roman copy of a Greek original sculpture from Pergamon, Asia Minor, showing a Celt committing suicide, having just killed his wife, rather than fall into the hands of his enemies. Dated to the late 3rd century BC. Together with *The Dying Gaul* (pp.194–5), it portrays the Mediterranean image of the Celt as 'noble savage', which was revived almost 2,000 years later by the European Romantic movement. (akg-images / Erich Lessing)

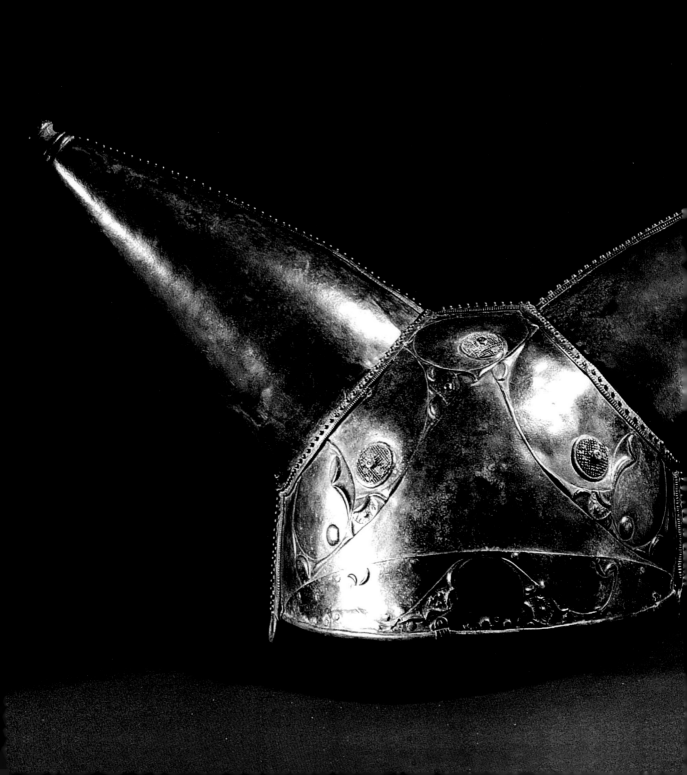

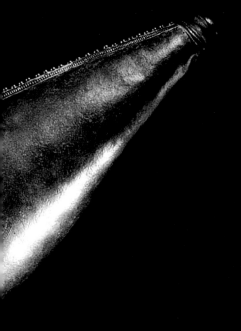

Part III
The Eagle and
the Raven

CHAPTER 6

THE CELTIBERIANS – ROME'S SPANISH ULCER

In ancient times, these two peoples, namely the Celts and the Iberians, fought among themselves over the land. But later they resolved their differences and settled down together, agreeing to intermarriage between their two peoples, and received the name Celtiberians. (Diodorus Siculus, Historical Library)

Until fairly recently, studies of the Celts have tended to neglect the Iberian peninsula. However, Iberia is the only place other than Gaul where the term 'Celt' is clearly mentioned in ancient sources. From the end of the 3rd century BC, the terms *Celtiberes* or *Celtiberi* were being used by classical authors. In fact, documentary information on the Celts in the Iberian peninsula is more extensive than for other regions, again with the exception of Gaul. A study of the sources reveals three distinct areas, located in the centre and the west of the peninsula, in which the presence of Celtic-speaking peoples is explicitly indicated: the eastern Meseta, the north-west, and the south-west. The Iberian peninsula in the Iron Age can be divided into two broad linguistic zones: the south and east facing the Mediterranean, inhabited by the non Indo-European-speaking Iberians, and the Celtic-speaking regions of the interior and Atlantic coast. The 'proto-Celtic' communities of the eastern Meseta were well placed to control the flow of trade from the metal-rich north-west to the Mediterranean, just as the Halstatt Princedoms had done between transalpine Europe and Italy. The Celtiberians probably emerged in much the same way, with the social elites adopting selected cultural elements from the Iberians whose own development as a distinctive culture owed much to wider Mediterranean contact. The result was a culture that was linguistically Celtic but which was significantly different materially from the Halstatt and La Tène cultures of central and western Europe.

A number of artefacts have been found in Iberia indicating that the influence of both Halstatt and La Tène cultures did spread south of the Pyrenees. However,

ATLANTIC OCEAN
CANTABRI
Ebro
Duero
VACCAEI
VETTONES
AREVACI
Numantia
CELTIBERIANS
Tagus
LUSITANI
Guadiana
IBERIANS
PYRENEES
HISPANIA CITERIOR
Emporion
Ilipa
Guadalquivir
BAETICA
HISPANIA ULTERIOR
Gadir
MEDITERRANEAN SEA

Main areas of resistance to Rome, 2nd century BC
Approximate limit of Roman domination, 200 BC
0   100 miles
0   200km

Iberia, showing the main areas of Celtiberian and Lusitanian resistance to Rome in the 2nd century BC.

neither was as widespread as elsewhere in transalpine Europe. It is also possible that groups of La Tène Celts may have migrated to the Iberian peninsula as settlers or mercenaries. Celtic war bands joined the Cimbri and Teutones in 104 BC when they briefly crossed the Pyrenees, while Caesar mentions the arrival of several thousand Gauls in the valley of the Ebro soon after the end of the Gallic War. Nevertheless, the impact on Celtiberian culture seems to have been minimal. The Celtiberians built strongly fortified hilltop settlements called *castros*, concentrated in the upper Douro valley. By the end of the 3rd century BC, a number evolved into large urban

Remains of the Celtic settlement at Castro de Coana, Villacondide, Spain. (Prisma / Ancient Art & Architecture Collection Ltd)

settlements, possibly influenced by the Iberians. They fulfilled a similar function to the oppida in Gaul and elsewhere in Celtic Europe. Numantia, one of the most important, was densely populated and, like Bibracte, had a regular street plan at the time of its capture by Rome in 133 BC.

Celtiberian culture spread from its heartland on the central Meseta to many other areas of the peninsula. The distribution of Celtic place name elements with the suffix *briga* ('fortified hill') or the prefix *seg* ('victory') indicates that Celtiberian influence extended across most of central and western Iberia. The peoples identified by classical authors were known by ethnic rather than by tribal names. It seems likely, therefore, that Celtiberian expansion was the result of the gradual 'Celtification' of neighbouring tribes, with the emergence of warrior elites rather than large movements of population. Increasing Celtic influence is also shown in dress and weapons, with evidence too of the adoption of the cult of the severed head. The Celtiberians had little direct contact with the Mediterranean until the mid-3rd century BC, when Carthage began to expand its influence and control over the peninsula. Large numbers were recruited into Carthaginian armies during the Second Punic War against Rome. Celtiberian mercenaries were later to fight on both sides when Rome intervened directly in Iberia. They were described as fearless, ferocious warriors who fought with a total disregard for their own safety.

Carthaginian power in Iberia was broken by Rome at the battle of Ilipa in 206 BC. The coastal areas from the Pyrenees to beyond the Pillars of Hercules were divided into two provinces, Hispania Citerior and Hispania Ulterior ('Nearer' and 'Further' Spain). The Celtiberians of the interior regained their independence. Rome's position in the peninsula was far from secure, however. Hostilities with the Iberian tribes, even within the new provinces, began almost immediately and quickly spread to involve the Celtiberians. Another 200 years passed before Rome was able to establish complete control over the entire peninsula. Polybius described the incessant conflict as 'a brushfire war', which was characterized not only by its ferocity but also by its unpredictable nature. Vicious fighting would alternate with periods of relative calm, when resentment and resistance would smoulder but could not be completely stamped out. The strength and morale of the legions were constantly worn down by the endurance of the Celtiberians who could not be decisively beaten in open battle. Their favoured, and extremely effective, tactic was to conduct a series of headlong charges at the Roman lines and then to suddenly withdraw in order to entice their enemy to break ranks and pursue them. They would then quickly rally and turn on those legionaries who had been foolish enough to follow and who had lost all discipline and formation. In this way they would maintain a constant pressure on the Romans throughout the day while preventing them from forcing the issue. Nightfall would bring a temporary respite since some tribes, particularly the Lusitani,

Gold brooch showing a naked warrior and his dog. The scabbard can be seen suspended on the right from the figure's sword belt. The sword blade and perhaps also a helmet plume are missing. The style is Hispanic and may represent a Celtiberian warrior. (Werner Forman Archive / British Museum)

who took a leading role in the war, believed it unpropitious to fight at night. The following day, however, the confrontation would begin again in the same way. Only winter slowed the conduct of operations, and even then not always.

The conquest and pacification of the Celtiberians by Rome is a catalogue of corruption and incompetence on the part of the civil and military authorities responsible for it. Military commanders and civil governors were more often concerned with making their own fortunes and reputations than striving for good governance. The rich natural resources of the Iberian peninsula, especially its mineral wealth, were a constant temptation for the greed of Roman administrators. Their attitude to the tribes was one of neglect and contempt. The most serious outbreaks of rebellion were always in response to the worst excesses, while the more peaceful interludes were always a consequence of the degree of mutual respect shown by both sides.

VIRIATUS AND THE LUSITANIAN WAR

Viriatus was a leader of the Lusitani, one of the most powerful Celtic-speaking groups of the western peninsula. Because of his stand against Rome, he has become a national hero in modern Portugal and Spain, in much the same way as Vercingetorix in France or Ambiorix in Belgium. Unlike them, he is said to have been of humble origins. However, given the position of warriors in Celtic society, it is probable that he was a man of some status.

The falcata, the infamous single-edged slashing sword used to devastating effect by the Celtiberians. (Photo Archive, Museo Arqueológico de Madrid)

In about 150 BC, efforts by the new Roman governor of Hispania Ulterior, Sulpicius Galba, to put an end to the persistent raids by the Lusitani on Roman territory led to yet another humiliating defeat for the legions. Rather than attempt to meet them in open battle again, Galba and his counterpart in Hispania Citerior, the governor Lucinius Lucullus, decided on a joint strategy of pillage and destruction.

This had the desired effect of forcing the Lusitani to agree on a truce: peace and farmland in exchange for surrendering their weapons. Some 30,000 Lusitani assembled. Separated into three camps, they laid down their arms. Galba then ordered his men to kill the warriors, who numbered about 9,000, and had the rest sold into slavery. News of the massacre caused disquiet even in the Senate, but Galba escaped prosecution even though he kept most of the profits from the operation. The scale of the atrocity provoked one of the worst uprisings that Rome ever had to face in Iberia.

Viriatus was among those who had escaped the massacre. Three years later, he was one of the principal Lusitanian leaders in the invasion of Hispania Ulterior. At the head of a large force of cavalry, his conduct and skill in preventing the Roman forces under Caius Vetilius from closing with the Lusitani enabled the invaders to evade the legions and withdraw successfully. For this, and his determination to resist subjugation to Rome at all costs, he was acclaimed overall war leader. Impatient to avenge his defeat, Vetilius returned to the offensive. Confident that his superiority in numbers would ensure victory, he led his army along the Guadiana River. The Romans again underestimated their enemy. Without bothering to send out an effective scouting force, Vetilius was unable to deploy his forces effectively when Viriatus ambushed them in a narrow pass. Vetilius was cut down with 6,000 of his men. His second-in-command withdrew, covering his retreat with Iberian auxiliaries. These too were caught and wiped out by the Lusitani as an example to all those who allied themselves with Rome.

Reinforcements were sent out from Rome to the peninsula. They served to make up the losses already suffered in the rebellion, but were not sufficient to put an end to it. Rome was now engaged in its final struggle against Carthage and was committing its main effort against its long-standing rival for hegemony in the western Mediterranean. All it could do in Iberia was to attempt to contain Viriatus

Elaborate bronze Celtiberian shield boss from Andalucía, Spain. This smaller, round shield known as a *caetra* was common among the Lusitani. (Photo Archive, Museo Arqueológico de Madrid)

149

and the Lusitani as best it could. Its best was not good enough, however. The Romans continued to lose men and, more importantly, the initiative. Viriatus exploited the situation by negotiating alliances with the Celtiberian tribes of the central Meseta. Roman garrisons were harassed; another army from Hispania Citerior was beaten. The morale of the legions fell even further. An anecdote by the governor of Hispania Citerior, Claudius Unimanus, paid tribute to the determination of the Lusitani and revealed the attitude of the Romans:

> In a narrow pass, 300 Lusitani faced 1,000 Romans. As a result of the action, 70 of the former and 320 of the latter died. When the victorious Lusitani retired, one of them on foot became separated and was surrounded by a detachment of pursuing cavalry. The lone warrior stabbed the horse of one of the riders with his spear, and with a blow of his sword cut the rider's head off, causing such terror among the others that they prudently retired under his arrogant and contemptuous gaze. (Cassius Dio, *History of Rome*)

Viriatus was at the peak of his success. The prestige he had gained in defeating the Romans time and again brought warriors flocking to his standard from all parts of the peninsula. The pendulum, however, had begun to swing back. In 146 BC, Rome finally crushed Carthage at the battle of Zama. The manpower and resources needed to subdue the Lusitani could now be made available.

In 145 BC, Fabius Maximus, a member of the great Scipio family who had played a leading role in the defeat of the Carthaginians in Iberia and in Africa, was appointed commander in Hispania Ulterior. At long last, Rome had a competent general in the peninsula. On taking up his command, he spent an entire year training his men and securing local cooperation, refusing to be provoked into action prematurely by the guerrilla tactics of the Lusitani. His efforts paid off. Viriatus was beaten in the first engagement and forced onto the defensive. It was the first Roman victory in the peninsula for almost ten years. A number of indecisive engagements followed. Viriatus avoided pitched battles, preferring the hit-and-run tactics of the charge and the feigned flight at which his warriors excelled. Nevertheless, the years of fighting had taken their toll on the Lusitani. Their effective strength was steadily falling, and Viriatus was forced to pull back to the Lusitanian heartland where he intended to recuperate and make up for his losses. The Romans took advantage of this lull to reoccupy and pacify those areas that he abandoned. 'Pacification' usually involved execution for the warriors and slavery for their families. The Roman advance into Lusitanian territory itself was met with fierce resistance. Then, unexpectedly, Viriatus offered peace terms. He demanded that the borders of

Sculpture of a Celtiberian warrior. Note the falcata and the typical Celtic long shield. The headgear remains something of a mystery: perhaps the crest represents the mane or tail of a horse. (Photo Archive, Museo Arqueológico de Madrid)

Lusitania be respected and that the Lusitani be granted the status of *amici populi romani*, 'Friends of the Roman People'; in other words, independent allies. The terms were agreed and referred back to Rome where they were ratified by the Senate.

Inevitably, the peace did not last long. The defeats and humiliation that Viriatus had inflicted on the might of Rome for so long could not be allowed to go unpunished. In 140 BC, the Romans began a series of operations which were designed

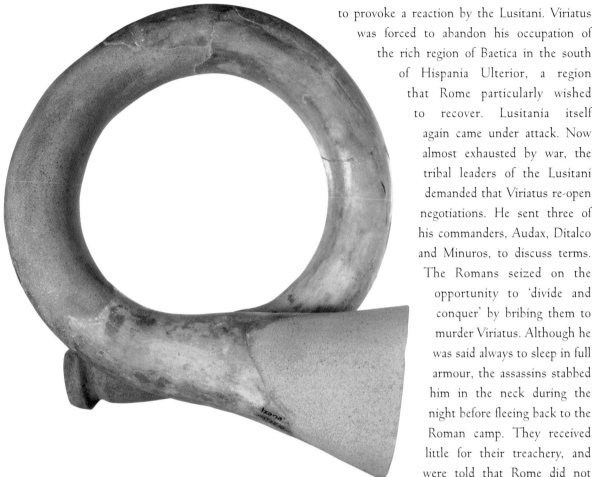

to provoke a reaction by the Lusitani. Viriatus was forced to abandon his occupation of the rich region of Baetica in the south of Hispania Ulterior, a region that Rome particularly wished to recover. Lusitania itself again came under attack. Now almost exhausted by war, the tribal leaders of the Lusitani demanded that Viriatus re-open negotiations. He sent three of his commanders, Audax, Ditalco and Minuros, to discuss terms. The Romans seized on the opportunity to 'divide and conquer' by bribing them to murder Viriatus. Although he was said always to sleep in full armour, the assassins stabbed him in the neck during the night before fleeing back to the Roman camp. They received little for their treachery, and were told that Rome did not reward traitors.

ABOVE AND OPPOSITE
Celtiberian ceramic war horns from Izana and Numantia. The wolf-headed model may have been attached to a tube like the Gallic and British carnyx. (Photo Archive, Museo Arqueológico de Madrid)

The Lusitani were devastated by the death of Viriatus. Without his skill and inspiration in war, they were unable to resist for very long. Perhaps the Romans had also learned something as a result of the rebellion since the Lusitani were subsequently treated with greater leniency than many other tribes.

THE SIEGE OF NUMANTIA

While Viriatus and the Lusitani threatened the province of Hispania Ulterior, the Celtiberians had inflicted further humiliating defeats on Roman forces in central Iberia. The death of Viriatus and the end of the Lusitanian war did not bring a respite in the north. In 137 BC, an attempt to take the Celtiberian stronghold of Numantia ended in 20,000 Romans being trapped and forced to surrender by 4,000 Celtiberians.

Numantia had been the object of attempted sieges by Roman forces on several previous occasions during earlier wars with the Celtiberians. As in the war against the Lusitani, Roman commanders continually underestimated their opponents and demonstrated an almost unbelievable level of ineptitude which time and again resulted in the ambush of entire armies and the death of thousands of Roman troops. The situation in the peninsula had become intolerable for Rome. In 134 BC, Rome's finest living soldier, Scipio Aemilianus Africanus, the victor of the battle of Zama and the grandson of the Scipio who had defeated Hannibal, was appointed consul of Hispania Citerior as an extraordinary measure in contravention of the constitution to reassert control and to repair the reputation of the army.

In May he began his campaign against Numantia. Under his command were 14,000 Roman and Italian troops, plus an equal number of local auxiliaries. Many of these came from the Iberian tribes of the Ebro valley, which had submitted to Rome. Their value and reliability was at best doubtful. Scipio approached Numantia by a circuitous route to avoid the most likely ambush sites and also to intimidate other tribes, such as the Vaccaei, who might normally be expected to actively support the Numantines.

The oppidum of Numantia is situated on a hilltop overlooking the confluence of the rivers Duero, Merdancho and Tera, about 9km (5½ miles) north of the modern Spanish town of Soría. In the mid-2nd century BC, it was one of the principal urban centres of the Celtiberian tribe known as the Arevaci. Today, the remains of its fortifications and buildings and the geometric layout of its streets can still be seen and bear witness to its wealth and sophistication. Archaeological excavations have revealed that it extended over 22 hectares (54 acres) with a resident population of perhaps as many as 10,000. Protected on three sides by water, the only practical line of approach for an attacker was from the north-east. The hilltop stronghold was defended by several lines of ramparts, reinforced at intervals by large round towers. Despite his superiority in numbers, Scipio decided against an immediate attempt to storm the oppidum. Lack of confidence in much of his army and the fearsome reputation of the Arevaci, especially now that they were defending their own territory, persuaded him that a siege was the best way to ensure victory. A temporary palisade was built, cutting off the open approach to Numantia from the north-east. Then, a stone wall of circumvallation was constructed right around the oppidum. It stretched for 9km (5½ miles), stood 3m (9ft 10in) high and was protected by a 3m-deep ditch on the inner side. Bridges carried it across the rivers that flowed around Numantia. On the outer side, 300 wooden towers, one every 30m (98ft 5in) or so, mounted light catapults. The wall linked seven fortified camps that were sited on high ground. Today, their impressive remains show the thoroughness with which they were laid out and the determination of the Romans to put an end to Celtiberian resistance.

The Numantines did not let these preparations go unhindered. The construction gangs had to be protected by detachments who stood under arms to fight off frequent attacks. Efforts were also made to force a passage past the most vulnerable points of the siege works, where they crossed the rivers, in order to bring in supplies and reinforcements. To counter this, Scipio had wooden booms with sword blades and spearheads embedded in them anchored between the riverbanks. With Numantia effectively cut off, conditions inside the oppidum steadily deteriorated throughout the following winter. As supplies dwindled and the inhabitants began to starve, a last desperate attempt was made to seek help to raise the siege. A small group of warriors scaled the Roman defences undetected at night, stole horses and made off for other towns of the Vaccaei. Fear of Roman reprisals outweighed the traditional bonds of clientage and loyalty, however, and their appeals went almost unheeded. A mere 400 young warriors from Lutia volunteered against the will of the ruling oligarchy. To protect the town and their own position, the rulers sent word to Scipio. The Roman commander promptly marched on Lutia and demanded the surrender of the rebels who had already fled. Threatened with the sack of their town, the Lutians handed over an equivalent number of innocent youths whose right hands were amputated *pour encourager les autres*.

A remarkable Celtiberian silver pectoral, 1st century BC, found at Chao de Lamas (Portugal). (akg-images / Nimatallah)

In the besieged oppidum, all hope of outside help was abandoned. In the late spring of 133 BC, the starving Numantines were obliged to send a delegation to negotiate with Scipio. Rome's terms were those it always demanded: unconditional surrender and the confiscation of all weapons. As always, the latter was totally unacceptable to the Celtiberian warriors, who considered this the denial of their status and manhood, the ultimate shame. Back in Numantia, the rage that this demand provoked was turned against the messengers themselves who were accused of treachery and collusion with the Romans, and were butchered for their pains. After nine months of siege, in July or August 133 BC, Numantia surrendered unconditionally. The Greek historian Appian claimed that the population had been reduced to cannibalism. He wrote that such was their love of liberty that many chose to commit suicide rather than capitulate. Families poisoned themselves, weapons were destroyed and the city itself was set on fire. The survivors were sold into

A Celtiberian shield boss of gold and silver, 1st century BC. (akg-images / Nimatallah)

slavery, except for 50 warriors who were chosen by Scipio to take part in his triumph in Rome. Numantia was razed and its reconstruction forbidden. Its territory was divided among its neighbours.

The fall of Numantia did not mark the end of resistance to Rome in Iberia, or Hispania as it now became known. The tribes of the Cantabrian mountains in the far north of the peninsula were only finally subdued at the end of the 1st century BC by an army led by the new Emperor Augustus. The tragic end of the struggle of the Celtic peoples of the Iberian peninsula was described by the Roman historian Cassius Dio:

> Not many of the Cantabri were taken prisoner, for when they saw that they had lost all hope of freedom, they also lost all desire to preserve their lives. Some set fire to their forts and cut their own throats; others willingly remained with their companions and died in the flames or took poison in sight of all. In this way, the great majority, and the fiercest among the warriors, were wiped out. (*History of Rome*)

CHAPTER 7

THE BATTLE FOR GAUL

Caesar found no unrest in Gaul; everything was absolutely quiet. This state of peace, however, did not last. First one war broke out against him of its own accord and then another was added, so that his greatest wish was fulfilled of waging war and winning success for the whole period of his command. (Cassius Dio, History of Rome)

With the destruction of Carthage in 146 BC, Rome's hegemony over the western Mediterranean was complete. The defeat of the Celtiberians at Numantia 13 years later ensured the security of the Republic's Hispanic provinces. To link them with the Italian province of Gallia Cisalpina, a safe overland route under Roman control was required.

The Greeks of Massalia had long been an ally of Rome. In 125 BC, the city appealed for help against the Saluvii, a tribe of mixed Celtic and Ligurian stock which controlled the coastal trade routes to the Alps. A Roman force was dispatched and duly defeated the Saluvii, burning their oppidum at Entremont. However, whereas on previous occasions they had been withdrawn, this time the legions stayed, establishing a military base called Aquae Sextiae. They then embarked on a campaign further north against the Allobroges who had supported the Saluvii, and then against their allies, the powerful Arverni to the west of the river Rhône. Within five years, Rome had annexed a vast swathe of territory stretching from the Pyrenees to the Alps and north along the Rhône valley. A colony was founded at Narbo (Narbonne) to secure the coastal plain west of the Rhône, while a road, known as the Via Domitia after the Roman commander Domitius Ahenobarbus, was built linking Rome's possessions in Italy and Hispania. The new province was called Gallia Transalpina, 'Gaul on the far side of the Alps'.

The defeats suffered by the Romans at the hands of the Cimbri and Teutones in their journey south from the Jutland peninsula at the end of the 2nd century BC

Gaul, showing the main
areas of Gallic resistance
and Caesar's campaign
against Vercingetorix
in 52 BC.

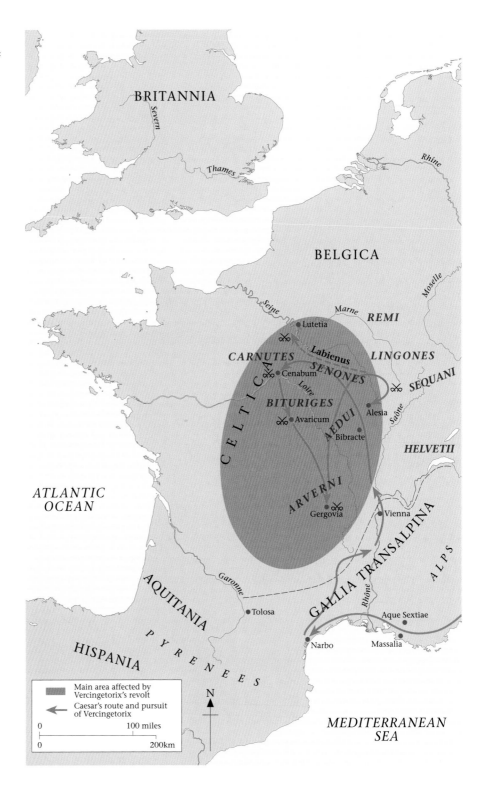

encouraged rebellion among the Gallic tribes now chafing under Roman rule. Many joined the migrating horde. Others, notably the Allobroges and the Volcae Tectosages of the south-west, whose ancestors had wandered across Europe as mercenary bands, took the opportunity to strike back at the Romans. The victories at Aquae Sextiae and Vercellae under the command of Rome's most able general, Gaius Marius, whose reforms had transformed the Roman army, enabled Rome to regain control. However, the province was the scene of continual unrest for the next 50 years as a succession of corrupt governors gave free rein to the virulent anti-Celtic prejudice of the Romans that dated back to the sack of Rome 300 years earlier. The Allobroges rebelled again and were subdued with great difficulty in 61 BC, but the Arverni remained a constant threat beyond the borders of Transalpina. To counter this, Rome entered into a formal alliance with one of the most powerful and prosperous tribes of Gaul, the Aedui, who were traditional enemies of the Arverni. Their lands in central Gaul, in modern Burgundy, were situated in the region through which flowed three of the country's main rivers, the Loire, the Saône and the Seine, giving them unrivalled control of a number of principal trade routes. The Aedui had actively encouraged Roman intervention in Gaul since before the founding of Gallia Transalpina. For their long-standing loyalty, they were granted the title of 'Brothers and Friends of Rome'. Inexorably, Rome was being drawn into the heart of the Celtic world.

In the 50 years following the invasion of the Cimbri and Teutones, Germanic-speaking peoples continued to migrate southwards, encroaching on Celtic territories north of the Alps. Their penetration of the upper Rhineland put pressure on the Helvetii, who had originally lived beyond the Rhine. Forced into what is now modern Switzerland, they sought to escape the constant threat from the Germans by a planned migration across central Gaul. The migration was meticulously prepared over three years and perhaps provides an insight into the Celtic migrations to Italy over 300 years earlier. The Helvetii planned to settle on the territory of the Santones, a tribe living in the west of Gaul near the Atlantic coast. Whether an agreement had been reached between them or whether the Helvetii intended to take the territory by force is uncertain. In the spring of 58 BC, when all was ready, the Helvetii began their journey, having burned their towns and fields and destroyed surplus grain. There would be no turning back. However, the movement of over 300,000 people (according to Caesar) would not pass unnoticed. The situation in central Gaul was already unstable. In the age-old feud between the Aedui and their neighbours to the north-east, the Sequani, the latter hired Germanic mercenaries from among the Suebi, the tribe responsible for much of the pressure on the

Helvetii, with a promise of land in return for their services. Under their king Ariovistus, the Germans mauled the Aedui before turning on their erstwhile employers. Further Roman intervention in Gaul was now inevitable. The Aedui appealed for help to the new governor of both Gallia Cisalpina and Transalpina, Gaius Julius Caesar.

Caesar was one of the three most powerful men in Rome at this time. Caesar, together with Gnaeus Pompeius Magnus ('Pompey the Great') and Marcus Licinius Crassus, conspired to control the state through what is known as the 'First Triumvirate', an unstable alliance in which they manipulated the republican constitution to further their own interests. Of the three, Caesar was in the weakest position, having neither the military reputation of Pompey nor the wealth of Crassus. He intended that his governorship of Gaul would provide both and at the same time increase his political standing.

The proposed route of the Helvetii would take them for a short distance through the territory of the Allobroges, into Roman territory. Caesar now had his chance to provoke a war with the Gauls. He refused their request to enter Transalpina and also warned them against entering the territory of the allied Aedui. When the Helvetii continued their route, avoiding the Roman province, Caesar pursued them and forced them to turn and fight while crossing the river Saône not far from the Aeduan capital at Bibracte. The defeat of the Helvetii was total. The survivors, barely a third of all those who had set out at the beginning of the migration, were sent back to the lands they had abandoned to rebuild their settlements. The Allobroges were ordered

Roman legionaries of the late Republic depicted on the Altar of Domitius Ahenobarbus. Caesar's troops would have been equipped like this. Note the mailshirts, which were adopted from the Celts. (akg-images / Erich Lessing)

to supply them with grain until they could feed themselves. It is clear from these arrangements that Caesar intended to use the Helvetii as a buffer against further German incursions across the Rhine. The Suebi under Ariovistus, who had occupied the territory of the Sequani the previous year, were Caesar's next target. They too were defeated in a single decisive encounter and expelled from Gaul.

Encouraged by his successes, Caesar determined to subdue the whole of Gaul. His task was made easier by the cooperation of a number of Gallic tribes, in particular the Aedui and the Remi, one of the principal Belgic tribes of northern Gaul. Caesar's campaign in 57 BC was directed against the other tribes of the Belgae. Of these, the Nervii were the most powerful and were described by Caesar as being particularly disdainful of others who had traded their courage in submitting to Rome. In alliance with the Atrebates and Viromandui, they gathered a host of over 60,000 warriors and lay in wait for Caesar's army as it advanced into Nervian territory. The legions came close to defeat following a surprise attack while they were making camp near the river Sambre, but were saved by their discipline and by Caesar's personal intervention in the fighting. The Belgae suffered heavy losses and were forced to surrender. A year later, Caesar campaigned against the Veneti and other maritime tribes of the Atlantic seaboard. Roman galleys built in the Loire estuary were able to overcome the powerful Gallic fleet as it lay becalmed in the Golfe du Morbihan, on the southern coast of modern Brittany. Between 55 and 54 BC, Caesar undertook two expeditions to Britain and made two forays across the Rhine.

Militarily, these latter campaigns were of little value, though the impact they had on popular opinion in Rome was spectacular: never before had a Roman general led the eagles so far beyond the civilized world. The timing was also ill-judged. In

Roman denarius struck at Narbonne, depicting the victory of Domitius Ahenobarbus over the Arverni under Bituitus. Dated c. 118 BC. (Werner Forman Archive / British Museum, London)

Caesar's absence, several of the tribes of the Belgae again rose in revolt, angered at the Romans' requisition of much of their grain stocks in a year of particularly bad harvests. Led by their leader, Ambiorix, the Eburones ambushed and massacred five cohorts of a newly raised legion on the march. Caesar gave a grim account of the battle, obtained from the very few survivors:

> The Gauls were equal to our troops in fighting quality and superior in numbers. Though their general had failed them and fortune had deserted them, our men trusted in their courage to save them. Every time a cohort charged, a large number of the enemy fell. Seeing this, Ambiorix ordered his men to throw their javelins without going too close and to give ground before the Roman charges. Being lightly armed and trained by daily practice to carry out such tactics, they were able to inflict heavy casualties. As soon as the legionaries began to retire to their main body, they were to follow up. These orders were strictly obeyed. Whenever a cohort charged, the enemy retreated. A temporary gap was of course left in the defensive formation the legion had adopted, so the next unit was exposed to missiles on its unprotected right flank. When the cohort began to fall back, it was surrounded by the Gauls who had given way before it. If the Romans tried to hold their ground in the line, they had no room for manoeuvre and were too bunched together to avoid the javelins that the Gallic host rained on them. (*The Conquest of Gaul*)

The Roman commander, Sabinus, who had already been deceived by Ambiorix into abandoning his camp with pledges of safe conduct, now sought to parley with the Eburones:

While he was discussing terms with Ambiorix, he was surrounded and killed together with the officers who had accompanied him. At this, the Gauls raised their customary shout of triumph and charged, breaking our ranks. Cotta [the second-in-command] fell fighting where he stood, and most of the soldiers with him. The survivors retreated to the camp from which they had come, withstanding the enemy's onslaught til nightfall. That night, seeing that all hope was lost, every man committed suicide. Those few who had escaped the battle made their way through the forest to Labienus' camp. (Caesar, *The Conquest of Gaul*)

The rebellion was put down with considerable difficulty and only after the region had been devastated by the Romans. The Eburones and their allies were said to have been almost exterminated.

THE REVOLT OF VERCINGETORIX

With the suppression of the rebellion of the Eburones, by the end of 53 BC Caesar's position seemed secure. He had secured domination over the Celts of Gaul through a careful strategy of divide and rule. Those tribes hostile to Roman intervention had been defeated or cowed into submission. He had crossed the Rhine and led the legions into Britain to deter Celtic interference in what had almost become his personal fiefdom. However, the rebellion of Ambiorix was a major blow to Caesar's strategy. It was the first clear Roman defeat in Gaul and did not go unremarked by other tribes, who were now coming to realize that only by putting aside their traditional differences and their ingrained custom of constantly waging war on each other could they hope to successfully resist ever-increasing Roman encroachment. Luxury goods that served to increase the prestige and status of the tribal elites were one thing; the choice between annihilation or total submission was quite another. Even the Aedui, who had remained loyal allies of Rome for over half a century, were reluctantly convinced that the point had now been reached when a stand must be made if Gallic independence were to be preserved. The leading members of many tribes of central Gaul met at the Aeduan capital Bibracte. Only the Remi and the Lingones stayed away – with the destruction of the Belgae their position between the rivers Seine and Marne was not only secured but enhanced. They had seen the consequences of the failed rebellion of their powerful northern neighbours. These factors weighed heavily in their decision to remain loyal to Rome.

Aware of the political unrest in Rome and the growing tension between Caesar and Pompey, the council at Bibracte decided to strike at once. They agreed to place overall command in the hands of a young chieftain of the Arverni named Vercingetorix. His name, if it is such rather than a title that he assumed, reflects his role. It can be translated as 'great warrior king' or 'great king of warriors'. His father was Celtillus who had been accused of conspiring to restore the monarchy and to have himself proclaimed king, for which he had been put to death. Believing that the situation in Gaul was calm, Caesar had returned to Cisalpine Gaul to deal with the administrative affairs of the province.

At the beginning of January 52 BC, the first blow was struck in Cenabum, the modern Orléans, the main oppidum of the Carnutes. Because of the importance of the territory of the Carnutes, which was considered to be the symbolic centre of Gaul, it has been suggested that the Druids played a leading role in organizing the revolt by persuading the tribes to cooperate. Hundreds of Roman citizens, most of them merchants and traders, were murdered, an example that was soon followed in towns and settlements throughout central Gaul. At the same time, Vercingetorix sent raiding parties south across the Cévennes mountains into Gallia Transalpina itself to harass the Romans and to encourage the Gauls there to join the rebellion. When news of the uprising reached Caesar he immediately returned, first to Narbo in order to counter the raids, and then north to rejoin his army, which was in winter quarters in the centre of Gaul. Taking Vercingetorix by surprise, Caesar crossed the Cévennes, still deep in snow, and

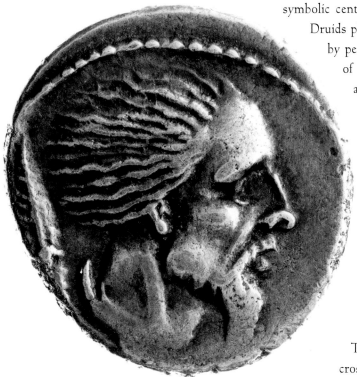

Roman coin minted in 46 BC to celebrate Caesar's victory in Gaul. Said to represent Vercingetorix, the portrait shows the archetypal Roman image of the barbarian Celt with lime-washed hair, flowing moustache and torc. A hero figure in a chariot appears on the reverse. (akg-images)

rode accompanied by only a small escort through Arvernian territory to the town of Vienna (Viennes, south of Lyon) where he was able to cross to the eastern bank of the river Rhône into safer territory.

Vercingetorix had failed in his first objective, to keep Caesar cut off from his legions. Rather than risk facing Caesar in open battle, he kept his forces on the move, adopting a scorched-earth policy by burning towns and farms to deprive the Romans of the grain that was stored there, which they badly needed at this early period of the year. Against his better judgment, Vercingetorix agreed to the pleas of the inhabitants of Avaricum (Bourges), the capital of the Bituriges, to spare the town, which they insisted was strong enough to withstand any siege. The Romans duly invested Avaricum. The confidence of the population was misplaced: their attempt to surrender after a siege of 27 days was rejected and the entire population of the town, said by Caesar to be some 40,000, was put to the sword. Vercingetorix retreated south into the heartlands of the Arverni, pursued by Caesar and six legions while four legions under the command of Caesar's most trusted subordinate, Titus Labienus, were detached to engage the Senones and Parisi along the valley of the Seine. Unable to outrun the Romans, Vercingetorix retired behind the massive fortifications of the principal oppidum of the Arverni at Gergovia, near the modern city of Clermont Ferrand.

The overgrown ramparts of the oppidum of Bibracte. (Author's collection)

Iron helmet recovered
from Alésia. (Musée des
Antiquités nationales, St
Germain-en-Laye, France
/ Bridgeman Art Library)

Iron helmet recovered from Alésia. (Musée des Antiquités nationales, St Germain-en-Laye, France / Bridgeman Art Library)

Without sufficient forces to undertake an effective siege, Caesar decided on a swift attack, trusting to the tenacity of his men to storm the ramparts. However, his plan degenerated into a series of uncoordinated attacks up the steep slopes of the hilltop oppidum and the Romans were driven back with heavy casualties. Caesar promptly withdrew to link up again with Labienus, who had also been forced to withdraw along the line of the river Seine from Lutetia, the modern Paris, having failed to secure his northern flank. This move was construed by Vercingetorix as a retreat. Although still unwilling to risk a battle in the open against the legions, he attempted to cut the Romans off from support or reinforcement from Italy by blocking their line of march. Caesar's account of the ensuing engagement reveals the emphasis now placed on elite cavalry units among many of the tribes of Gaul:

The whole of [Vercingetorix'] cavalry, numbering some 15,000 men, was ordered to concentrate at Bibracte. He said that he would content himself with the infantry which he had from the previous campaign and would not tempt fortune by fighting a pitched battle. With his great cavalry strength it would be quite easy to prevent the Romans from getting corn and forage …

Meanwhile, Caesar had found a way of remedying [his] inferiority in cavalry. Since all the roads were blocked and no reinforcements could be got from the Province or from Italy, he sent across the Rhine to the German tribes which he had subdued in previous campaigns, and obtained some of their cavalry attended by the light infantrymen who always fought among them. As their horses were unsuitable for the service required of them, he mounted the Germans on horses requisitioned from the military tribunes and other Romans of equestrian rank, as well as from time-expired volunteers.

During all this time, the Gauls were concentrating the troops which had been operating in the territory of the Arverni and the cavalry levied from all over Gaul. A large number of cavalry had now been assembled … Vercingetorix … summoned his cavalry commanders to a council of war and addressed them saying that the hour of victory had arrived … The cavalrymen shouted that they should swear a solemn oath not to allow any man who had not ridden twice through the enemy's column to enter his home again or to see his wife, children or parents. This proposal was approved, and every man was duly sworn.

Next day their cavalry was divided into three sections, two of which made a demonstration on either flank of the Roman column while the third barred the way of the vanguard. Caesar

The oppidum of Gergovia from the south-east. Caesar's main attack was made uphill from the right. (Author's collection)

Aerial view of the site of Alésia from the south-west. One of Caesar's main camps was situated on the hillside in the centre background. (© Archéologie aérienne René Goguey)

also divided his cavalry into three sections and ordered them to advance against the enemy. Simultaneous engagements took place all along the column, which halted and formed a hollow square with the baggage inside. If Caesar saw the cavalry in difficulties anywhere or particularly hard pressed, he moved up some of the infantry and formed line of battle which hindered the enemy's pursuit and encouraged the cavalry by the assurance of support. Eventually the German horse gained the top of some rising ground on the right, dislodged some of the enemy and chased them with heavy loss to a river where Vercingetorix' infantry was posted. At this, the rest of his cavalry fled, afraid of being surrounded, and were cut down in numbers all over the field …

After the rout of his cavalry, Vercingetorix withdrew his troops from their position in front of the camp and marched straight for Alésia, an oppidum of the Mandubii … Caesar … followed the enemy as long as daylight lasted and killed some three thousand of their rearguard. The next day he camped near Alésia. The Gauls were terrified by the defeat of their cavalry, on which they particularly relied. (*The Conquest of Gaul*)

OPPOSITE Statue of Vercingetorix, Alésia. (Author's collection)

Vercingetorix withdrew to Alésia with some 80,000 men. As expected, Caesar followed up. This time, he had his full force at his disposal and proceeded to blockade the entire town as Scipio Aemilianus had done at Numantia. He ordered the construction of a line of fortifications to be built around Alésia, cutting it off from the outside. This line of circumvallation extended 18km (11 miles) and stood 4m (13ft 1in) high. Wooden towers were constructed at regular intervals. On the inner side two ditches, each 4.5m (14ft 9in) wide, were dug, that nearest the fortifications filled with water from the nearby rivers. These were fronted by pits with sharpened stakes and thorn bushes. The siege works were completed within a month. Caesar's description has been verified by archaeological excavations first carried out in the mid-19th century. The Gauls tried to prevent Alésia from being completely cut off. When it became clear that they would not succeed, Vercingetorix sent part of his cavalry to break out and summon a relief force. To guard against this, Caesar ordered the construction of a second line of fortifications to protect his army from any threat from outside. The line of contravallation, outside the first, stretched 21km (13 miles). The besiegers would now become the besieged in their turn.

Conditions inside Alésia rapidly deteriorated, with the local population of the town and Vercingetorix' army competing for the dwindling stocks of food. The Gallic leader decided to send the women and children out of the citadel with a request to Caesar to allow them to pass through the Roman siege lines. Refusing to cede any advantage to the Gauls, Caesar gave orders that nothing was to be done for these unfortunates, who were left to starve in the no-man's land between the ramparts of the oppidum and the line of circumvallation. The pitiful sight and cries of their abandoned families caused the morale of the Gauls to plummet, just as Caesar had intended, and there were even calls to surrender among the Mandubii. The arrival of the Gallic relief force, estimated to be about 100,000 strong, though Caesar claimed it to be as many as 250,000, commanded by the Atrebaten leader and Caesar's former ally Commius, gave the besieged garrison new hope. As Commius launched an attack on the outer Roman line, Vercingetorix attempted to break out from Alésia. The battle lasted all day but by sunset the Romans had managed to drive back both attacks. The Gauls regrouped and two days later attacked again under the cover of night. Surprised, Caesar was temporarily forced to abandon a section of his line. Only the swift response by the Roman cavalry led by Mark Antony prevented Commius from breaking through. The inner line was also attacked again but, in the dark, the pits and ditches delayed Vercingetorix' men, giving the Romans sufficient time to rush reinforcements to the threatened sector. Caesar's men were almost at the end of their tether:

Reconstruction of Roman
fortifications at Alésia,
L'Archéodrome, Beaune.
(Author's collection)

deprived of adequate supplies since the beginning of the campaign and now
under siege themselves with food rationed even further, the combined attacks of
Vercingetorix and Commius had sapped their strength.

The following day the Gauls made a further attempt to break the siege of Alésia.
Led by a cousin of Vercingetorix, Vercassivellaunus, a massive assault by some 60,000
men was launched on the weakest point in the Roman fortifications, an area to the
north-west where the lie of the land prevented the construction of a continuous wall.
Once again, the assault was made in coordination with Vercingetorix' forces who
assaulted the Roman inner line at the same spot. Vercassivellaunus' force breached the
outer line of fortifications. Their shouts of triumph could be heard throughout the
oppidum. Caesar sent Labienus with six cohorts (about 2,500 men) to help stem the
tide of Gallic warriors who were now streaming into the Roman encampment between
the siege lines, while he led a counter-attack against the inner offensive. His presence
galvanized the legions. The Gauls were forced back and the inner line was held.
However, the sector held by Labienus was on the verge of collapse. The Roman
defence was being overwhelmed as thousands of Gauls pressed against the breach. The
outcome of the battle for Alésia hung in the balance. In desperation, Caesar took
personal command of his remaining cavalry reserve, in total about 6,000 horsemen,
leading them outside the siege lines to charge the Gallic relief force in the flank and

rear. His gamble paid off. Within moments, the attack by Vercassivellaunus' men disintegrated; those inside the walls were slaughtered, those outside were cut down as they tried to retreat.

From the citadel, Vercingetorix witnessed the final defeat of his armies. It was also the end of any hope of continued independence for the tribes of Gaul. His own men were starving; the relief force was either dead or scattered. There would be no further help from outside. The next day he rode out of Alésia alone and surrendered to Caesar, allegedly casting his weapons at the Roman's feet and stripping off his armour before kneeling in submission. Perhaps considered a traitor because of his past service with Caesar's forces, he was taken to Rome and left to rot for six years in the infamous Marmetine prison until Caesar was finally able to stage his triumph for his victory in Gaul. After the procession, the former Gallic leader was ritually strangled, a human sacrifice to the might of Rome. The remainder of the garrison of Alésia and the survivors of the relief force who had been taken prisoner were sold as slaves. The Aedui and Arverni were exempted. They were released as a gesture of good will by Caesar in order to secure the renewed alliance of these powerful tribes, whose cooperation and influence among their clients was essential if Rome was to re-establish its control in Gaul. The battle of Alésia marked the end of organized resistance to the Roman domination of Gaul, although a number of actions took place in 51 BC, notably the siege of Uxellodunum in the far south-west of the country. With its fall the Gallic War was finally over.

The seven years of incessant war from 58 to 51 BC had devastated the heartland of the Celtic world. From a population estimated to be three million at the start of Caesar's campaigns, it is thought that up to one million died or were enslaved. Economically, Gaul took 50 years to recover; politically, it was never the same again. Those who, like Commius, refused to accept the loss of their independence had only one option left open to them: exile to Britain, the last Celtic land that was still free of the shadow of Rome.

CHAPTER 8

BEYOND THE OCEAN

There is a two-day journey by ship to the Holy Island, so-called by the ancients. The island is large in extent and lies between the waves. The race of the Hierni live there. The island of the Albiones lies not far away. (Avienus, Ora Maritima)

To the ancient Greeks and Romans, Britain was a land shrouded in mystery that lay on the very edge of the world in the great Ocean River. In the second half of the 6th century BC, the Greek author Hecataeus of Miletus wrote of an island across the sea from the land of the Celts that was believed to be as large as Sicily. The poem *Ora Maritima*, 'The Sea Shores', quoted above, was composed by the Latin poet Avienus in the 4th century AD. It referred to a number of much earlier texts, including the *Massilliot Periplus*, a description of the sea routes around the Atlantic coast of Iron Age Europe from southern Iberia to Brittany, Ireland and Britain. In the 5th century BC, the Carthaginian Himilco was the first known explorer from the Mediterranean to venture out to the islands 'beyond the ocean'. He reached the Isles of the Oestrymnides, probably the islands off the south coast of Brittany. The natives here traded with the islands of Albion and Ierne, two days' sailing to the north. In the late 4th century BC, the Greek Pytheas of Massalia explored the Atlantic coasts as far north as the legendary Ultima Thule (Iceland), sailing right round the coast of Britain in the process. The observations that Pytheas made during this remarkable voyage were later used by Diodorus Siculus, who wrote the following:

The inhabitants of Britain who live around the promontory of Belerion are especially hospitable to strangers and have adopted a civilized manner of life because of their contacts with traders and other peoples. They work tin into pieces the size of knuckle bones and transport it to an island which lies off the coast called Ictis. On the island, traders buy the tin

Route of Boudica's army
Cities sacked by Boudica's army
Counter march by Paulinus and XIV Legion
Agricola's invasion of Caledonia

0   100 miles
0   200km

Mons Graupius?
AD 85

CALEDONES

Inchtuthil

Antonine Wall

Hadrian's Wall

BRIGANTES

MONA

AD 60

Trent

ICENI

ORDOVICES

Severn

TRINOVANTES

AD 60

BRIGANTES

MANAPII

Shannon

SILURES

CATUVELLAUNI

Verulamium

Camulodunum

Thames

Londinium

ATREBATES

REGNI

Maiden
Castle

N

Britain, showing the
areas affected by
Boudica's rebellion,
and Agricola's campaign
against the Caledones
in the 1st century AD.

from the natives and take it from there across to Gaul. Then, making their way overland, they bring their goods by packhorse to the mouth of the river Rhône. (*Historical Library*)

The British Isles had a long history of trade in metals with mainland Europe (especially in tin, essential for the production of bronze), which were exported by sea from south-west Britain to Tartessian and later to Phoenician trading ports on the Atlantic coast, and overland through Gaul to the western Mediterranean. The promontory of Belerion is thought to be the Lizard Point in Cornwall and the island of Ictis, St Michael's Mount. If this is so, the most likely route taken by the tin traders may have been around Armorica to the Oestrymnides near the Loire estuary. The Veneti of southern Brittany were reputed to be particularly experienced seamen, possessing large sea-going vessels that were capable of regularly navigating the dangerous waters around the Armorican peninsula and across the Channel.

Diodorus employed the term *Pretannia*, Latinized from Pytheas' *Pretannike*, to describe the country, and *Pretani* for its inhabitants. *Pretani* is generally believed to mean 'painted' or rather 'tattooed', very likely referring to the use by the Britons of the blue dye extracted from woad. As such, it is more likely to be a nickname given them by outsiders, probably the continental Celts, rather than a term used by the natives of Britain to describe themselves. It may be compared with the word *Picti*, the Picts, which was used by the Romans in the 3rd century AD to describe the peoples beyond the frontier in northern Britain. It has also survived in Welsh as the name for Britain, *Prydein*, as well as the Roman *Britannia* and the modern 'Britain'. The names Albion and Ierne are certainly Celtic and were probably used by the inhabitants themselves. Our first reliable eye-witness account of Britain and its inhabitants comes from Caesar's reports of his two expeditions from Gaul in 55 and 54 BC:

> The interior of the country is inhabited by people who regard themselves as indigenous to the island; the coastal areas by peoples who had migrated from the lands of the Belgae, who are still called after the tribes from whom they originated and who came to plunder and then to settle. The most civilized are those who inhabit Cantium whose customs differ little from those of Gaul. Most of the interior tribes do not grow corn but live on milk and meat. (*The Conquest of Gaul*)

Caesar's observations that groups of Celts had migrated to Britain from the Continent and had settled among the indigenous Celtic-speaking peoples are supported by evidence from tribal names and the archaeological record. The Belgae and the Atrebates of central southern Britain and the Parisi of Yorkshire all had connections in northern Gaul. According to Caesar, Diviciacus, a chieftain of the Belgic Suessiones, also ruled over parts of Britain, recalling the Celtic custom of clientage, not only between individuals but also between tribes. The Belgae were once thought to have migrated to Britain between the late 2nd and early 1st centuries BC. Some probably did, given the unsettled conditions in Gaul resulting from the migration of the Cimbri and Teutones, and the increasing confrontation between Gauls and Romans following the creation of the Roman province of Gallia Transalpina. However, artefacts of continental and even Danubian origin dating from the 3rd century BC strongly suggest that the Belgae crossed to Britain at about the same time as they settled in northern Gaul. This was no large-scale invasion but rather the arrival of fairly small warrior groups that quickly integrated into the elite of the local communities. The graves of the Parisi, for example, have revealed a number of continental artefacts, in particular the remains of elaborate two-wheeled chariots, although the bodies were buried according to local custom.

Relating to Ireland, a map by the Greek geographer Ptolemy, who lived in the 2nd century AD, confirms that the Mediterranean world had at least some knowledge of the land the Romans called *Hibernia*. This map shows not only the most significant features of the Irish coastline, but also the names of some of the principal tribes. The mention of the Brigantes and the Manapii is particularly interesting, since the former is the namesake of the powerful confederation in northern Britain, while the name of the latter is almost identical to that of the Menapii, a Belgic tribe of northern Gaul. It is quite possible, therefore, that Ireland was also affected by the great Celtic migrations of the 3rd century BC. The medieval Irish *Book of Invasions* describes the traditional coming of the Gaels and the Fir Bolg to Ireland, which might be a distant folk memory of the arrival of the Belgae and other continental Celtic warrior groups. Nevertheless, archaeological evidence does not support large-scale immigration of Celtic-speaking peoples to either Britain or Ireland during the Iron Age.

This 1st- or 2nd-century BC bronze boss is all that remains of a Celtic shield that was found in the Thames at Wandsworth, probably thrown there as an offering to the gods. It is decorated with two large birds whose wings develop into tendril motifs. (Werner Forman Archive / British Museum, London)

The richly decorated Desborough mirror, with its chased and engraved abstract patterns, is a fine example of insular La Tène art. The plain bronze face would have been highly polished. (Werner Forman Archive / British Museum, London)

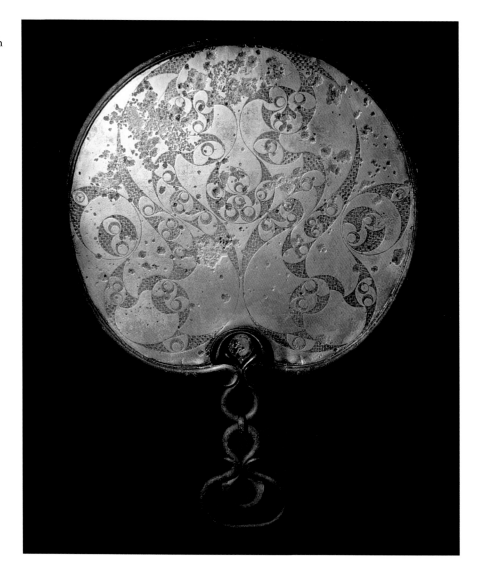

Despite Strabo's comment that its inhabitants were even more savage than the Britons and that they routinely indulged in cannibalism, Ireland was neither isolated nor unknown. Tacitus reported that its climate, and the character and material culture of its inhabitants, were much like those of Britain. Its coast and harbours were quite well known from traders. As far as we are aware, Agricola was the only Roman general to have considered an expedition there. During his campaign in the Scottish Lowlands he estimated that the country could be taken and held with a single legion and a strong force of auxiliaries. Given the effort required by the Romans to invade and occupy Britain, this seems to be a wildly optimistic assessment.

By the 1st century BC, the Celts of southern and south-eastern Britain differed little from their relatives and neighbours across the Channel in terms of material culture and social, economic and political development. City states were evolving; fortified oppida such as those at Camulodunum and Verulamium (St Albans) had become centres of power comparable to continental urban sites. Coinage had been adopted from continental styles. Inscriptions in Latin have preserved the names of kings and nobles, including Commius, king of the Atrebates, and Cunobelinos of the Catuvellauni, who centuries later became the model for Shakespeare's Cymbeline.

CAESAR'S EXPEDITIONS

On the morning of 27 August 55 BC, a fleet of 80 ships carrying two Roman legions – approximately 10,000 men – under the personal command of Caesar himself lay at anchor off the coast of Britain. Above them towered the white chalk cliffs near the future harbour of Dover. Lining the clifftops stood thousands of British warriors in full battle array. In search of a suitable place to land, the Roman fleet sailed several miles north-east along the coast, but were followed by part of the British host. The Romans attempted to run their ships ashore on the flat shingle beach at Deal, but were unable to do so because of their deep draught. The Britons, meanwhile, advanced into the shallows, daring the Romans to leave the safety of their ships. Intimidated by the unfamiliar situation, the legionaries hung back, unwilling to attempt a landing in deep water, which would hamper them in engaging the enemy. It was at this point that the *aquilifer*, the bearer of the eagle standard of Caesar's favoured Legio X, is said to have thrown the eagle into the ranks of the enemy and jumped overboard after it, shouting to others to follow him. The thought of the disgrace of losing the most sacred symbol of the legion to the Britons overcame the reluctance of the Romans, who leapt from one ship after another and fought their way ashore.

The Britons were driven off, but Caesar was unable to pursue them without his cavalry contingent, which had not yet arrived. The beachhead was consolidated and defended, with many ships drawn up on the shore. A truce was arranged with the Britons, who undertook to provide hostages. Four days later the transports carrying the Roman cavalry were sighted. However, as they approached, a violent storm broke out scattering them and forcing some back across the Channel. The storm pounded the ships riding at anchor, driving them ashore and severely damaging those already beached. Deprived of cavalry support, Caesar's options were now extremely limited. Any advance inland that might have been planned was now impossible; even foraging was extremely risky. The Romans set about salvaging what

The White Cliffs of Albion, Caesar's first view of Britain. (© Ric Ergenbright / CORBIS)

they could from the wreckage of their fleet. The Britons, meanwhile, seeing the precarious position of the would-be invaders, disregarded the truce and began to bring up reinforcements with the intention of pushing the legions back into the sea. Unable to make a direct assault on the fortifications of the Roman camp, they maintained a constant harassment of Roman patrols and the foraging parties that were sent out to seize vital corn supplies. After several days, Caesar deployed his forces in front of the camp to entice the Britons into attacking him on his own terms. The Britons charged but were unable to break the Roman line. They fell back in disorder and then broke and ran as the legionaries followed up in pursuit. The following day the Britons again sent ambassadors to negotiate terms. They were anxious to be rid of the Romans and Caesar realized that his situation was untenable. He could not afford to be cut off from events in Gaul by the approaching winter. He demanded twice as many hostages as originally agreed and, with all but 12 of his ships pronounced seaworthy, re-embarked the legions and departed.

Caesar established his winter quarters in the territory of the Belgae, in north-west Gaul. Few of the hostages promised by the Britons arrived. Caesar used this as the main reason behind his decision to return to Britain the following year, although it is more than likely that he saw a further opportunity to enhance his personal standing and was determined to make a better showing than on the first expedition.

In early July 54 BC, a fleet of over 800 ships sailed from Gesoriacum (Boulogne), carrying five legions and 2,000 cavalry. As on the previous occasion, they landed near Deal. This time they were unopposed. Caesar marched with the bulk of his forces in pursuit of the Britons, who withdrew inland. They made a stand at a ford on the river Stour, probably near the modern Canterbury, but were forced to retire to the fortified oppidum of Bigbury. With some difficulty, the Legio VII took the hillfort. The Britons retreated again while Caesar decided against a further advance in unfamiliar country. That night another violent storm blew up the Channel, again wrecking many of his ships. Before any further operations could be launched, the beachhead had to be consolidated once more and major repairs undertaken. In the meantime, the Britons temporarily overcame their inter-tribal rivalries and appointed Cassivellaunus, king of the powerful tribe that was later known as the Catuvellauni, as overall commander against the Romans. The Britons again took up a position on the line of the river Stour, but after a hard-fought battle Cassivellaunus was forced to conduct a fighting retreat in the direction of the Thames. From prisoners and deserters, Caesar learned that the Thames could be forded in one place and only with difficulty. The Britons lined the far bank, which was also defended by sharp wooden stakes above and below the water line. However, the élan of the legions and Roman cavalry carried them across the river with such determination that Cassivellaunus' army put up only a token resistance before breaking off the battle and retreating into the surrounding woods.

The bulk of the British forces was dismissed, or perhaps more likely simply melted away as faith in their leader's ability to defeat the Romans was lost. Cassivellaunus retained 4,000 charioteers, possibly his own retinue for the most part. In the wooded terrain north of the Thames, he adopted hit-and-run tactics that the Romans found difficult to counter, and a scorched-earth policy to deprive them of food and supplies. However, old rivalries were reasserting themselves. Tribes that resented the power and domination of the Catuvellauni, in particular the equally powerful Trinovantes, began to make overtures to Caesar in return for protection against Cassivellaunus. Through them, he learnt the location of the stronghold of the Catuvellauni, probably the hillfort at Wheathampstead, near the modern St Albans. The Britons were once again unable to withstand the legionary assault, though Cassivellaunus evaded capture. In a bold move, he sent word to his allies in the south-east to mount an attack on the Roman base camp on the coast in an attempt to dissuade Caesar from any further advance. The attack failed. In the face of so many losses, the devastation of his territory and the desertion of erstwhile allies, Cassivellaunus sent envoys to Caesar to negotiate a surrender. The terms were moderate. Caesar had received news of renewed unrest in Gaul and, conscious of the lateness of the season and of the unpredictability of the weather, was anxious to make the Channel crossing in the best possible conditions. Cassivellaunus was commanded to provide hostages as a guarantee of his conduct and was forbidden to make war on the Trinovantes, who were now under the protection of Rome.

Caesar left Britain in early September. The return to Gaul was again disrupted by bad weather and had to be conducted in two stages because of the numbers of prisoners and the loss of some ships in the previous storm. The Romans did not return for almost a century. When they did, it was not merely a reconnaissance in force but a full-scale invasion. Much of the planning for this was done on the basis of the information gathered by Caesar on the nature of the terrain and the inhabitants of Britain, and on their political and military customs.

Bronze horse mask from northern Britain, dating to the 2nd century BC, perhaps used as parade armour for a chariot pony. (National Museum of Scotland, Edinburgh)

THE CLAUDIAN INVASION

For almost a century Britain remained free of direct Roman influence. Civil war and efforts to subdue the German tribes beyond the Rhine prevented any further Roman attempt to occupy the island after the death of Caesar. Economic ties with the new Roman Empire increased, however, as Britain became one of the principal sources of grain supplies for the Rhine garrisons. Gold, silver and iron, as well as the inevitable slaves, were also exported from Britain.

A similar pattern of economic and political evolution to that in Gaul prior to Caesar's campaigns can be seen in central and southern Britain, with the development of city states around powerful tribes. Despite Caesar's defeat of the Catuvellauni, and the protection extended to their rivals, the Trinovantes, the former continued to dominate the rich south-east of the country. The Catuvellauni, now ruled by Cunobelinos, took over the territory of the Trinovantes in the early years of the 1st century AD, making the principal oppidum, Camulodunum, their own. In so doing, they were in a more favourable position to control cross-Channel trade, much of which was now conducted via the Thames estuary. Within a generation, the Catuvellaunian power had spread south of the Thames. The Cantiaci of Kent seem to have become a client tribe, while parts of the northern territories of the Atrebates were also annexed. The Atrebates were ruled by Verica, a descendant of Commius the Atrebatan from northern Gaul, who had fled to Britain after siding with Vercingetorix against Caesar. The struggle between the two most powerful tribal groupings in southern Britain provided the motive for renewed Roman intervention.

Cunobelinos was succeeded by his sons Caratacus and Togodumnus in about 40 AD. They defeated Verica, who fled to Gaul. His appeal to the new Emperor Claudius for Roman assistance against the Catuvellauni, and the arrogant demand by Caratacus for his immediate return, could not have come at a better moment. Claudius had been proclaimed emperor by the Praetorian Guard in the wake of their assassination of his predecessor, his insane nephew Gaius Caligula. Claudius was considered a political nonentity, which he may have been, and a fool, which he most certainly was not. The Praetorians viewed him as a temporary solution or, at best, a means to maintain their own power and influence. In order to keep his throne and possibly his life as well, Claudius needed some way to continue paying lavish handouts to the Praetorians and at the same time to consolidate his position in the eyes of the army and the people of Rome. An invasion of Britain would provide the solution.

Gold coin from Britain bearing the abbreviated name of Verica, king of the Atrebates, dated to the 1st century AD. (Werner Forman Archive / British Museum, London)

Bronze plaque found in a hoard at Stanwick, North Yorkshire. Possibly intended as a chariot decoration, its flowing lines form an abstract image of a horse's head. (Werner Forman Archive / British Museum, London)

Unlike Caesar's expeditions to Britain, there is no first-hand account of the Claudian invasion. We are reliant upon evidence from archaeological remains and the description by the historian Cassius Dio, writing over 150 years later. An army of four legions, about 20,000 men, and perhaps as many auxiliaries, set out from Gesoriacum under the command of Aulus Plautius. Their unopposed landing is traditionally located at Richborough, on the north-east coast of Kent. A different view has been put forward in recent years in favour of a landing further west near the modern city of Chichester in West Sussex. This was an area ruled by Verica and therefore could presumably be considered friendly territory. Without naming the landing site, Cassius Dio does say that the Roman fleet sailed in three divisions. Later operations in the south-west might support the idea that one of them landed on the south coast. On balance, the weight of evidence still seems to favour the traditional site. The Romans needed to engage and defeat the main forces of the Catuvellauni, and to move quickly to occupy Camulodunum. Certainly, reinforcements and supplies came in via Richborough, which became one of the most important Roman ports in Britain.

The Romans advanced to a river, identified as the Medway, where Plautius' Batavian auxiliaries from the Rhine delta swam across undetected to take the Britons by surprise in the flank. Their main target was the chariot and cavalry horses. With the loss of much of their mobility, the Britons retired after a hard-fought battle. As Cassivellaunus had done before him, Caratacus withdrew to the north bank of the Thames somewhere near the City of London. Once again, the Romans were able to force a passage without great difficulty, dispersing the Britons who took shelter in woods and marshland. Plautius then halted his legions to await reinforcements and the emperor himself, who arrived accompanied by a number of elephants. Now in personal command of the campaign, Claudius oversaw the final advance on Camulodunum. His triumph complete and his position consolidated, at least for the moment, Claudius lost no time in returning to Rome. With the defeat of the Catuvellauni, a number of tribes either surrendered or placed themselves under the protection of Rome. While Plautius consolidated his position in the south-east, he

Heavy bronze bracelet
decorated with enamel
and coloured glass from
Perthshire, Scotland,
1st or 2nd century AD.
(Werner Forman Archive
/ British Museum,
London)

sent the Legio II Augusta, under the command of Vespasian, to the south-west in order to secure the region. Vespasian subdued the Durotriges of present-day Dorset, successfully storming the formidable defences of the hillfort of Maiden Castle.

Caratacus had escaped the debacle and had fled across the river Severn to the lands of the Silures. Under his inspiration, resistance to the Roman occupation grew. Widespread rebellion was timed to coincide with the arrival of a new governor, Ostorius Scapula, in AD 47. Swift action on the part of Scapula defeated the Iceni in Norfolk and dissuaded other tribes who had been hesitating between peace and war. Further west was a different matter. Using the rugged landscape of modern Wales to its best advantage, the Silures, the Ordovices and the Deceangli stubbornly resisted the assaults of the legions. Tacitus provides an extensive description of the type of warfare waged by the Britons and the Roman response:

> The army then marched against the Silures, a fierce people and now full of confidence in the might of Caratacus, who by his many successful battles had proved himself to be far above the other generals of the Britons. Inferior in military strength, but with the advantage of the terrain, he resolved on a final confrontation. He selected a position for the engagement in which advance and retreat alike would be difficult for our men and comparatively easy for his own. On the hillsides, wherever they could be approached by a gentle slope, he piled up rocks to serve as a rampart. A river of varying depth was also to his front. His forces were drawn up behind these defences.

The chieftains of the several tribes went from rank to rank, encouraging and raising the spirit of their men by making light of their fears, and other warlike encouragements. As for Caratacus, he was everywhere, declaring that the coming battle would either be the beginning of the recovery of their freedom, or of everlasting bondage. He appealed to the memory of their forefathers who had driven out the dictator Caesar and by whose valour they were still free from the Roman yoke. While he spoke, the British host raised a great cry and every warrior bound himself by oath to shrink from neither weapons nor wounds.

Their fervour intimidated the Roman general. The river to his front, the rampart the Britons had added to it, the frowning hilltops, and the masses of fighting men all daunted him. But his prefects and tribunes insisted on battle, exclaiming that valour could overcome all things, and similarly inspired the ardour of the troops. Having surveyed the strong and weak points of the position, Ostorius led his men across the river without difficulty. As they approached the barricade, our soldiers suffered heavy casualties from the enemy's missiles. Then they closed ranks and formed the testudo. The crude barrier of stones was torn down and they advanced to engage the Britons hand-to-hand. The barbarians retired to the heights but were pursued vigorously by our auxiliaries and the legions, the former harassing them with missiles, while

An unusual torc from northern Britain, perhaps modelled on Roman pearl necklaces, 1st century AD. (Werner Forman Archive / British Museum, London)

the latter closed with them. Without the shelter of their barricade and with most lacking armour and helmets, the Britons were utterly broken. It was a glorious victory: the wife and daughter of Caratacus were captured, and his brothers surrendered. (*Annals*)

Caratacus escaped again and sought refuge among the Brigantes, a powerful tribal confederation in the north of Britain. The Brigantes were divided over their attitude to Rome. One of their principal leaders, Venutius, favoured resistance. His wife, Cartimandua, a women with great status and influence in her own right, wished to strengthen her own position by coming to an accommodation with the invaders. She had Caratacus seized and delivered to the Romans in chains. Nine years after the invasion, thousands turned out to see him paraded through Rome where his fame had preceded him. Claudius astutely treated him as an honourable foe and not only spared his life but granted him a villa and a pension.

In Wales, the Deceangli, the Ordovices and the Silures continued to resist Roman attempts to subdue them for the next decade. The final struggle came when a new governor, Suetonius Paulinus, decided to mount an operation against the heart of British resistance, the Druidic holy island of Mona, and at the same time destroy the power of the Celtic priesthood and intellectual class. In his account of the campaign, Tacitus gives a vivid description of the enemy that the legions faced:

> On the shore stood the opposing army with its dense ranks of armed warriors. Between the ranks women dressed in black ran back and forth like Furies, their hair blowing wildly, waving fire brands. All around, the Druids raised their arms to the heavens screaming dreadful curses. Our soldiers were terrified by the unfamiliar sight and stood motionless as if paralysed. (*Annals*)

At Paulinus' urging, the Roman troops advanced across the shallows of the Menai Strait. As they did so, their fear turned to anger. They cut down the defenders, warriors, Druids and priestesses alike. Then, following Caesar's example in Gaul, they destroyed the sacred groves.

One of a pair of bronze bridle bits recovered from a peat bog in Galway. Decorated with stylized foliage, it may have been used to harness a chariot pony. Dated to the 2nd or 3rd century AD. (Werner Forman Archive / National Museum of Ireland)

BOUDICA'S REBELLION

Away from the shifting frontier, Roman civil administration began to function. In order to free more serving soldiers for his operations in the west, Scapula had established a colony of veteran legionaries at Camulodunum. There they could farm the land given to them by a grateful empire and at the same time act as a defence force to deter any opposition in the occupied areas. The British elite was often left in nominal control of their tribal areas and encouraged to adopt Roman culture and lifestyles. These 'client kings' were allowed to continue to rule on condition that they kept the peace and paid the taxes imposed by Rome.

Two such client kings were Togidubnus, the heir of Verica the Atrebaten, who may have been responsible for the building of the magnificent villa at Fishbourne in Sussex, and Prasutagus, king of the Iceni whose territory extended across modern Norfolk and parts of Suffolk and Cambridgeshire. Those responsible for administering Rome's conquests were concerned not only with ensuring that the emperor received an appropriate income from his new subjects, but also, and perhaps more importantly, that they should themselves profit from their appointments. In other words, the system was used and abused to the growing disenchantment and anger of the native populations. Perhaps in an effort to safeguard his family and people, Prasutagus named the Emperor Nero, Claudius' successor, as joint heir to his kingdom with his two daughters. In this he failed. On his death in AD 59 or 60, the fragile independence of the Iceni was brutally ended. Prasutagus' wealth was seized; it is said that his daughters were raped and his widow, Boudica, flogged. The nobility was dispossessed and the people enslaved.

The response of the Britons was immediate and overwhelming. The Iceni appealed to their neighbours the Trinovantes, who had seen their capital Camulodunum expropriated by Roman veterans and were themselves victims of the greed of the procurator Decianus Catus, the province's chief financial officer. Led by Boudica, thousands of Britons headed south towards Camulodunum in search of revenge. The terrified colonists appealed to the procurator for help. The 200 men he sent from Londinium were absurdly inadequate, and Camulodunum was quickly overrun and sacked. Some soldiers and civilians took refuge in the temple of the now deified Emperor Claudius, a particular object of hatred as the symbol of Roman tyranny. The Britons razed it to the ground. The Legio IX, understrength and marching to relieve Camulodunum, was ambushed and destroyed. Boudica and the British host descended upon Londinium, from where Catus fled to the safety of Gaul.

On hearing of the rebellion, Paulinus cut short his operation against Mona and marched south with the XIV and XX legions, sending orders to the Legio II stationed in the far south-west, near present-day Exeter, to join him at Londinium. Inexplicably, these orders went unheeded. Arriving with his cavalry, Paulinus realized that the town was impossible to defend. He ordered it to be abandoned and withdrew north again along Watling Street to rejoin his legions.

Londinium had developed rapidly since the invasion. By AD 60, its population was perhaps as high as 10,000. Many fled as the Britons approached. Like Camulodunum, the town was sacked and its inhabitants butchered. Recent excavations have revealed a layer of burnt debris and scorched timbers marking the devastation. A similar fate was inflicted on Verulamium, the capital of the Catuvellauni. Although they had played a leading role in resisting the initial invasion, they had since reached an

Gold torc from Knock, County Roscommon, Ireland. It has similarities in design with the continental Waldalgesheim style and is considered to be one of the earliest indications of the introduction of La Tène art in Ireland. Dated to the 3rd century BC. (Werner Forman Archive / National Museum of Ireland)

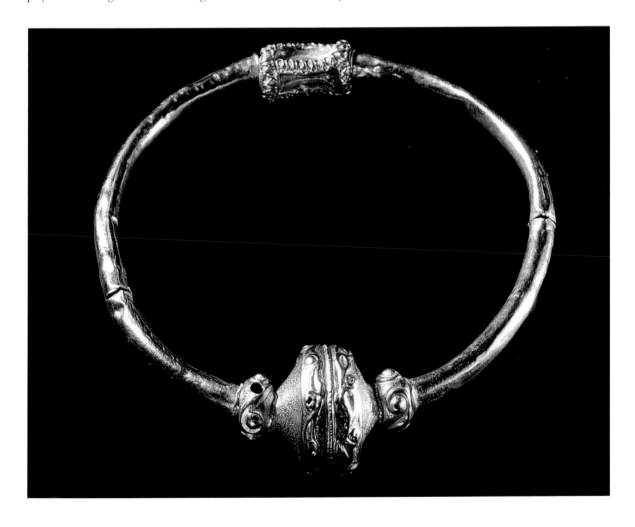

Modern reconstruction of a British war chariot based on archaeological finds, descriptions and pictorial references. More recent studies suggest that the floor was supported by leather straps attached to the loops on the sides of the vehicle, thus providing a simple and effective form of suspension.
(© Trustees of the British Museum / PS300290)

accommodation with Rome. This, and the ancient rivalry between them and the Trinovantes, made the town an obvious target. In all, it has been estimated that some 70–80,000 people, Romans and Britons, were slaughtered in Camulodunum, Londinium and Verulamium. Boudica's army was not interested in taking prisoners; their one aim was to avenge themselves on the Roman occupiers and those native Britons whom they saw as collaborators and traitors.

Rome's authority in Britain had virtually collapsed; the ability of the empire to retain control of its new province stood on a knife edge. With no sign of Legio II, Paulinus would have to face Boudica's host, estimated by one Roman source to be over 200,000 strong, with a mere 10,000: the XIV and XX legions, and auxiliaries from local garrisons. Whatever the number of the Britons, they included not only warriors but also their families, women and children, together with a vast train of wagons. In order to counter the Britons' numerical superiority and to reduce the mobility of their chariots and cavalry, Paulinus deployed his forces to take the best advantage of the terrain. He chose a position in front of a defile between surrounding hills, with open ground to the front and the protection of a dense wood in the rear. The site of the battle that decided the fate of Roman Britain is unknown. The traditional theory puts it near Mancetter in Warwickshire. However, a more recent alternative favours a location closer to Londinium not far from Towcester in Northamptonshire, where the terrain seems to correspond more closely to the description given by Tacitus.

Led by Boudica riding in a chariot with her daughters, the Britons closed in on the Romans. She went along the battle line overseeing the deployment of the tribes. Behind them, the mass of wagons formed a grandstand for the camp followers to witness their victory. Both Tacitus and Cassius Dio provide vivid accounts of the battle:

> At first the legions held their position, keeping to the narrow defile as a defence. When they had exhausted their missiles, which they discharged with unerring aim on the approaching foe, they advanced swiftly in a wedge-like column. The auxiliaries attacked in a similar fashion, while the cavalry with their lances broke through all who offered a strong resistance. (Tacitus, *Annals*)

> The battle took many forms. Light-armed troops exchanged missiles with light-armed, heavy-armed were opposed to heavy-armed, cavalry clashed with cavalry, and Roman archers engaged the chariots of the barbarians. The Britons charged the Romans with their chariots, sweeping them aside, but, since they fought without breastplates, would themselves be repulsed by volleys of arrows. Horsemen would ride down infantrymen and infantrymen would strike down horsemen. A group of Romans formed in close order would advance to meet the chariots, while others would be scattered by them; a band of Britons would come to close quarters with the archers and rout them, while others were content to dodge their shafts at a distance. The struggle went on for a long time, both sides being animated by the same determination and daring. But finally, late in the day, the Romans prevailed. (Cassius Dio, *Roman History*).

As the Britons began to retreat they found their way blocked by the baggage train. Chaos and panic ensued as the warriors and their families sought to escape. The Romans spared neither in their pursuit. Tacitus claimed that nearly 80,000 were killed in the battle and the rout, for the loss of only 400 of Paulinus' men. Boudica fled and, like other defeated Celtic leaders before her, committed suicide by taking poison. She was mourned deeply by the Britons, who gave her a sumptuous burial.

Reinforcements from the Rhine garrisons and famine among the tribes that had rebelled ensured the pacification of southern Britain. The Roman presence was never again seriously challenged from within the province. Paulinus was made a scapegoat and relieved of his command. It is perhaps an indication of just how close Boudica came to forcing the Romans out of Britain that the policy of Paulinus' successor as governor was one characterized by inactivity and accommodation with the Britons.

AGRICOLA AND THE BATTLE OF MONS GRAUPIUS

Further efforts to bring the remainder of Britain under Roman control were delayed by the civil war that broke out in Rome following the overthrow of Nero in AD 68. The enthronement of Flavius Vespasianus (Vespasian), the commander of Legio II at the time of the Claudian invasion, as emperor by the Senate a year later marked the beginning of a period of strong and efficient government in the empire, and a renewal of campaigns against recalcitrant tribes in the troubled province of Britain. Both the Silures and the Ordovices were brought to heel at last, and the Brigantes were forced to accept Roman rule after the final defeat of Venutius, the ex-husband of Cartimandua.

In AD 78, Gnaeus Julius Agricola was appointed governor of Britain. He had previously served under Paulinus during Boudica's rebellion and later as commander of Legio XX. His experience convinced him that unrest among the Britons could be largely avoided if they were treated fairly and that a peaceful and prosperous province was as much in the Britons' interest as in Rome's. He set out, on the one hand, to rid the civil administration of injustice and abuse, and, on the other, to encourage the British nobility in particular to adopt the trappings of Roman society. In the field he was regarded as an able and humane commander.

Agricola's campaigns in Britain took him further north than any previous Roman commander. Following the subjugation of the tribes in the Lowlands of modern Scotland, he established a defensive line of forts across the narrow strip of land separating the estuaries of the rivers Forth and Clyde. Using these to protect his rear, he advanced into the region known to the Romans as Caledonia. As the legions, accompanied by British mercenaries and other auxiliary troops, marched roughly north-east with the Grampian mountains to their left, a Roman fleet kept pace with them, exploring the coast and seeking out suitable harbours to ensure adequate logistical support. In the face of Agricola's determination to subdue the entire island of Britain, the various Highland tribes formed an alliance under the command of Calgacus, a leader of the Caledonii, one of the most powerful peoples of the region.

He gathered an army said to be some 30,000 strong and confronted the Romans at the battle of Mons Graupius. The site of the battle is, once again, unknown. The traditional location is the hill of Bennachie in Aberdeenshire, although recently a strong argument in favour of a site not far from Perth has been put forward.

Agricola's forces numbered about 20,000, including 8,000 auxiliaries and 3,000 cavalry. The lighter troops formed the first line with the cavalry on the flanks and the legions behind them in reserve. The Caledonii and their allies deployed on the slopes of the hillside opposite them with their chariots manoeuvring between the lines. Tacitus described the battle as follows:

> The action began with an exchange of missiles. The Britons showed both steadiness and skill in parrying our javelins with their huge swords and small shields while raining volleys on us. Then Agricola ordered forward five auxiliary cohorts to engage them at close quarters. These veterans were well trained in close combat unlike the enemy who were at a disadvantage with their small shields and unwieldy swords which are not pointed and are quite unsuitable in a hand-to-hand struggle. The auxiliaries, raining blow after blow, striking them with their shield bosses and stabbing at their faces, pushed back the enemy on the flat ground and advanced up the hill. This encouraged the other cohorts to vigorously attack the enemy nearest to them. Many were left behind half dead, some even unwounded, in the pace of the advance. Meanwhile, our cavalry had routed the British chariots and had joined the infantry battle. Their first attack was terrifying but the dense ranks of the enemy and the rough ground soon brought them to a halt. The position of our infantry was precarious; they were jostled by our own horsemen while runaway chariots and riderless horses came plunging into their ranks from all sides.
>
> The Britons on the hillside who had so far taken no part in the battle saw that they outnumbered the Romans and began to move down to envelop our forces. However, Agricola had been expecting such a move and sent four squadrons of cavalry which he had kept in reserve to intercept them. The British charge was turned back in disorder. The tactics of the Britons now turned against them. Our cavalry rode round them and fell on their rear, wounding some, taking others prisoner, and then killing them as the Britons tried to rally. On the British side whole groups, even though they were armed, fled before inferior numbers; others, though unarmed, deliberately charged to a certain death. Even the vanquished now and then recovered their fury and courage. When they reached the woods, they rallied and ambushed the first rash pursuers. The over-confidence of our men might have had serious consequences, but Agricola ordered the auxiliaries to flush them out on to our cavalry. Seeing our troops reforming, the Britons turned and ran. The pursuit went on until nightfall and our men tired of killing. (*Agricola*)

The casualties from the battle were reported to be 360 Romans and about 10,000 Britons, most of whom would have been killed in the pursuit in the same way as Boudica's defeated army.

Following the battle, it was proclaimed in Rome that Agricola had finally subdued all the tribes of Britain. However, the uneasy peace of the next few decades contradicts this. The construction of the 'Glen Forts' at the entrances to the Highland glens and the huge legionary fortress at Inchtuthil in Perthshire would seem to imply an attempt to fence in an enemy who was still undefeated. Agricola may have won the battle of Mons Graupius but the failure to neutralize the potential threat to Roman security in northern Britain was to have serious consequences for the future.

Bronze statue of Boudica and her daughters, Victoria Embankment, London. (R. Sheridan / Ancient Art & Architecture Collection Ltd)

GALATA MORENTE
COPIA DA ORIGINALE BRONZEO
DI ARTE PERGAMENA (240-197 A.C.)

Part IV
Twilight

CHAPTER 9

THE THREAT FROM THE NORTH

... the Arverni and the Sequani hired some German mercenaries to help them [in their struggle for supremacy against the Aedui]. A first contingent of about fifteen thousand crossed the Rhine; but when the uncivilized barbarians had acquired a taste for life in Gaul with its good land and high standard of living, more were brought over until there were at present about 120,000 of them in the country.
(Caesar, The Conquest of Gaul)

PREVIOUS SPREAD
The Dying Gaul. Roman copy of a Greek original from Pergamon, Asia Minor, late 3rd century BC. It portrays the Mediterranean image of the Celt as 'noble savage', which was revived almost 2,000 years later by the European Romantic movement. (akg-images / Erich Lessing)

At the end of the 2nd century BC, the Celtic heartlands of transalpine Europe were faced with a more immediate threat than the growing power of Rome: the expansion of Germanic-speaking peoples from the north. This first became apparent about 120 BC, when the Cimbri from the Jutland peninsula, in modern Denmark, were forced from their homes by persistent flooding caused by climate change. They migrated south-east, accompanied by various groups known as the Teutones, a generic term for 'peoples' or 'tribes'. A substantial number of Celts also joined the migration, in particular the Ambrones from the low-lying coasts of north-west Europe. Moving into Bohemia, they came up against the most powerful Celtic tribe in central Europe, the Boii, who forced them to turn aside towards the kingdom of Noricum, where they invaded the territory of the Taurisci. The Taurisci had been allies of Rome for many years. However, the legions sent to support them were defeated by the Cimbri and Teutones near the city of Noreia on the Danube in 113 BC. Although the Alpine passes to Italy were now open to them, they chose to move west along the northern flanks of the Alps towards Gaul. As they approached the Celtic heartlands, other Celts and Germans swelled their numbers even more. In Gaul, this massive host defeated Roman armies sent against them time after time. In 105 BC, at the battle of Aurasio (Orange) in the province of Gallia Transalpina, they utterly destroyed the largest Roman army sent into the field since the war against Hannibal. It was also the costliest defeat since Cannae. News of the disaster at Arausio shook the Roman Republic to its foundations. The *terror cimbricus* became a watchword, as Rome expected the Cimbri

Bust of the Roman
general Gaius Marius
(157–86 BC). (Ancient
Art & Architecture Ltd)

and Teutones at its gates at any time. In this atmosphere of panic and desperation, an emergency was declared. The constitution was set aside and Gaius Marius, the victor over the Numidian king Jugurtha and Rome's most able general, was elected consul for an unprecedented, and technically illegal, five years in a row, starting in 104 BC.

Still the Cimbri and Teutones did not move into Italy. Instead, in 103 BC, they crossed the Pyrenees and ravaged the north of Iberia. The following year they returned to Gaul. Italy was now their objective. They split their forces, with the Teutones and Ambrones intending to cross into Italy through the western Alpine passes while the Cimbri would do so from further north. The Teutones were forced south by a Roman army commanded by Marius, who brought them to battle and defeated them at Aquae Sextiae, the modern Aix-en-Provence. The Cimbri, however, had passed through the Alps into northern Italy unopposed. The local Roman commander retreated behind the river Po to await the arrival of Marius. At Vercellae, near the confluence of the rivers Po and Sesia, in 101 BC, the Cimbri were caught between the two Roman forces and annihilated. Many of their woman were said to have killed themselves and their children in order to avoid slavery.

The migration of the Cimbri and Teutones was at one time presented as the main reason for the development of oppida in central and western Europe. But, as we have seen, this was the result of a process of social, political and economic evolution that had begun long before. Moreover, no significant archaeological trace of this migration has been found. Whether its scale and significance were exaggerated by Roman writers cannot be determined. It is probable, however, that the Roman vision of the event was coloured by previous experience of invasion from the north and the *terror gallicus*.

The Germans continued to move south, encroaching on lands that had been Celtic for over half a millennium. One of the areas first affected was that north of the river Main, from where Ariovistus invaded eastern Gaul in the 70s BC and from where other tribes threatened the Helvetii. After repelling the migration of the Helvetii, the Gauls requested Caesar's aid in removing the Germans under Ariovistus, who were occupying the territory of their former employers, the Gallic Sequani. With memories of the incursion of the Cimbri and Teutones still fresh, Rome was as keen as the Gauls to ensure that the Germans remained on the far side of the Rhine. Further east, Celtic Thuringia seems to have remained unaffected for almost another century. At about the same period, the Germanic confederation known as the Marcomanni invaded Bohemia, destroying the great oppidum at Závist near Prague. Moravia was also occupied by the German-speaking Quadi.

At the same time as the Germans were expanding south into central Europe, the Celts of the middle Danube were also coming under pressure from another aggressive people, the Dacians. Related to the Thracians, they originated from what is now Romania. They began to expand westwards across the Carpathians into Transylvania towards the end of the 2nd century BC, absorbing the native Celtic populations. Around 60 BC, under their king Burebistas, they attacked and defeated the Boii, Scordisci and Taurisci in northern Hungary and Slovakia. Archaeological evidence has revealed the violent destruction of the gates of the oppidum at Bratislava and of Dacian-style pottery in the ruins. Many Celts fled to take refuge with the Helvetii, supporting them in their attempt to migrate into Gaul.

Roman expansion north of the Alps did not occur until after the civil wars that brought the Republic to its violent end. The powerful Celtic kingdom of Noricum constituted a convenient buffer state controlling the passes through the Austrian Alps, as well as being an important exporter of iron. It was annexed in 15 BC when the new Emperor Augustus decided to bring the Alpine tribes under direct Roman rule. The conquest of Illyricum and Pannonia (the modern Croatia and Serbia) and Hungary followed between 12 and 9 BC. With the arrival of the Romans on the Danube at the end of the 1st century BC, the destruction of the independent Celtic world was virtually complete.

Coin depicting Vercingetorix, the celebrated leader of the Gauls against Caesar. (akg-images)

CHAPTER 10

THE END OF THE CELTIC WORLD

'If you review all the wars that Rome has waged, none has ended in a shorter time than that with the Gauls. Thenceforth, there has been unbroken and loyal peace. Mingled as they now are with us in their way of life, their culture, and by intermarriage, let them bring us their gold and their wealth rather than keep it in isolation'... Claudius' speech was followed by a decree of the Senate, and the Aedui were the first to be granted the right to enter the Senate. (Tacitus, Annals)

By AD 100, the Celtic world, which for half a millennium had encompassed much of Europe from the Atlantic to the Balkans, was gone. Of all the Celtic-speaking lands only Ireland and Scotland remained free of the domination of Rome, while beyond the Rhine and the Danube Germanic and Dacian tribes ruled unchallenged.

The La Tène artistic style, and the Celtic languages that had characterized and defined Celtic culture, faded away in the face of the classical civilization and its cultural values imposed by Rome. Romanization was slow to begin with, especially in Gaul after the devastation of Caesar's conquest. Traditional ways of attaining and expressing status and wealth, especially through military prowess, were now forbidden under the new *Pax Romana*. The Celtic elite was encouraged to adopt the Roman lifestyle of the Mediterranean urban aristocracies and its status symbols. Fine buildings, both public and private, now proclaimed rank and position in society; the education of children in schools replaced the custom of fostering; the feast gave way to the theatre and the games. Clientage remained, however, since it was as much a part of Roman society as that of the Celts. The Romanization of the Celts was greatly facilitated by the development of an urban society among many Celtic tribes in the last two centuries BC. Existing institutions, such as the election of ruling magistrates, were easily adapted to Roman political forms. The urban aristocracies were permitted to keep their property and privileges, and were encouraged actively to participate in local government. Roman citizenship, the ultimate status symbol, together with its political opportunities

and exemption from taxation, was granted to those who accepted and supported the new regime.

The bearing of arms had always been the right of every free man in Celtic society. To surrender them to a conqueror was perhaps the most difficult thing for the Celts to accept. For those who could or would not, there were two choices: exile or become a mercenary in the army of the enemy. This latter choice also provided a solution for those who still sought glory on the field of battle. It was an arrangement that suited both sides. The Celt could pursue the way of the warrior in the time-honoured manner as a mercenary. For the Romans, a potential source of resentment and possible rebellion would be deployed far from his home, where his desire to fight could be channelled in other provinces or on the frontiers of the empire. Celtic horsemen had always enjoyed a high reputation, and many young nobles joined auxiliary cavalry units. During their time with the eagles they were immersed in Roman culture and could also aspire to citizenship upon discharge.

The remains of Hadrian's Wall at Walltown Crags, Northumberland.
(© Sandro Vannini / CORBIS)

The transformation of Celtic society under the impact of the Roman conquest was by no means uniform. The Hispanic Celts were absorbed fairly quickly because of the existing links with the urbanized Mediterranean coastal region. Gaul was likewise easily assimilated due to the influence and example of the province of Gallia Transalpina. In Britain the picture is much less clear. Far from the Mediterranean world, it retained a distinct character of its own that set it apart from the continental Celts. Intensive agriculture and centralized states were rare beyond southern Britain; urbanization was rarer still. To the north and west, the country was sparsely populated and more loosely organized; agriculture was subsistence level and in places less important than flocks and herds. This contrast between the so-called 'highland' and 'lowland' zones of Britain can be seen in the Claudian invasion of the 1st century AD. Whereas the south and east up to a line running from the Severn estuary to the Wash were quickly overrun, Wales and the north of England were not subjugated for almost a generation. Despite a determined effort, Caledonia resisted attempts at occupation and was finally physically excluded from the empire. No expedition was ever mounted against Ireland. By the end of the 1st century AD Rome's economic and military resources had reached the limit of their capacity to expand the empire any further. The aggressive, offensive strategy that Rome had pursued since the foundation of the Republic over 500 years before was replaced by a defensive policy designed to preserve its gains and protect its frontiers.

In Britain, this was achieved, with a varying degree of success, by the construction of Hadrian's Wall. Built on the orders of the Emperor Hadrian following his visit to Britain in AD 122, the Wall was the most heavily fortified border in the empire. It runs for 80 Roman miles (17km) between the estuary of the river Tyne in the east to the Solway Firth in the west. Apart from the Wall itself, the frontier consists of vast earth banks and ditches on either side, 16 major fortresses and 'milecastles' at intervals of 1 Roman mile (1.4km) along its length. Construction is believed to have taken ten years. Archaeological evidence indicates that the Wall was successfully stormed on a number of occasions. However, it was never intended to be an impenetrable barrier. Its main purpose was to deter raids by hostile tribes from the north and to regulate, rather than prevent, movement across the frontier. The Wall was garrisoned by auxiliary units who would call on the support of the legion based at York in cases of large-scale incursions. Throughout the entire Roman period, three legions were always based in Britain, stationed in three great fortresses at Caerleon, Chester and York, stategically sited to dominate the Celtic north and west. Together with their supporting auxiliary troops, the total number of troops accounts for almost one-eighth of the entire Roman imperial forces. The presence of such a large garrison

OPPOSITE Housesteads, one of the main fortresses on Hadrian's Wall, Rome's north-west frontier in Britain. (© Jason Hawkes / CORBIS)

is testimony to the Roman perception that much of Britain was never fully pacified and that the native Britons could still pose a threat to the province.

The extent of the Romanization of Britain is still the subject of debate. It was certainly far less than in Gaul, where the last traces of Celtic social structures had vanished by AD 300 and the Gaulish language itself was all but extinct by AD 500. The so-called 'Celtic revival' in Britain in the 5th and 6th centuries AD, between the end of centralized imperial civil and military rule and the establishment of the early Anglo-Saxon kingdoms in what is now England, was the result of the Romano-British peoples being obliged to revert to local municipal government based on the former tribal entities, which still aspired to Roman ideals, rather than a conscious desire to return to a pre-Roman Celtic past. The name which they gave themselves, *combrogi*, can be translated as 'fellow citizens' or 'fellow countrymen', which hints at a continued common identification with their former status as Roman citizens. The term has been preserved in *Cymru*, the Welsh name for modern Wales.

Those parts of the Celtic world that were incorporated into the Roman Empire gradually adopted a new identity and a new language. As a result, any consciousness of a common identity that may have previously existed among the Celtic-speaking peoples of Iron Age Europe died out almost entirely during the Roman period. Only in the remote west, where the authority of Rome was weak or absent entirely, as in Brittany, western Britain, Scotland and above all Ireland, did Celtic languages and culture survive. To what extent the peoples of these areas regarded themselves as Celts is extremely difficult to say. There is certainly no indication that they did so. However, the cultural resurgence that was largely inspired by the distinctive form of 'Celtic' Christianity in Ireland in the early Middle Ages ensured the survival of myths, legends and art forms that symbolize the belief systems and behaviour patterns within Celtic society. Through them, we possess our most valuable link with the ancient Celtic world.

CHAPTER 11

ROMANCE AND REALITY

Anything is possible in the fabulous Celtic twilight. (J. R. R. Tolkien)

REDISCOVERING THE CELTS

For almost 1,500 years the ancient Celts faded from history. Knowledge of their existence lay hidden in copies of classical manuscripts in the libraries of Christian monasteries until the Renaissance of the 14th and 15th centuries brought renewed interest in Greek and Latin texts. The invention of printing made them available again, in the original or in translation, to scholars throughout western Europe, many of whom were interested in the historical origins of their own countries. The first to write about the Celts was the Scottish historian George Buchanan. In his *Rerum Scoticarum Historica*, published in 1582, Buchanan suggested that the Celts were a people who originally lived in southern Gaul from where they had migrated first to Iberia and then to Ireland and Scotland. Others had migrated directly from Gaul to Britain.

The modern view of the Celts can be traced to the publication in 1707 of the *Archaeologia Britannica* by the Welsh antiquarian Edward Lhuyd. In this work, Lhuyd outlined the similarities between Welsh, Gaelic, Cornish and Breton with the language of ancient Gaul. He referred to this group of related languages as 'Celtic', from *Celtae*, Caesar's name for the tribes of central Gaul. At that time, none of the Celtic-speaking peoples of the British Isles, or of Brittany, are known to have regarded themselves as Celts, but by the mid-18th century, 'Celtic' was being applied not only to the languages but also to the people who spoke them. Shortly after the publication of Lhuyd's *Archaeologia Britannica*, the Act of Union between England and Scotland created the United Kingdom of Great Britain. The Welsh, who

Early scholars mistakenly attributed Stonehenge to the Druids, although modern-day Druids still gather at the site to celebrate the summer solstice. (© Adam Woolfitt / CORBIS)

considered themselves the true descendants of the ancient Britons, objected to the term 'Great Britain', and the newly revived concept of the Celts provided a way for them to emphasize their own identity. Their example was followed by the Gaelic-speaking Irish and Scots, the Cornish and the Bretons in an attempt to maintain their distinctive identities in the face of increasing political and cultural domination by their English and French neighbours.

The 'rediscovery' of the Celts also had an impact beyond those searching for a historical identity. The classical barbarian stereotype of the Greeks and Romans was resurrected as the Celt became 'the noble savage' of the Romantics, whose art and literature reflected their opposition to the philosophers of the Enlightenment and to the growing pollution of the countryside brought about by the nascent industrial revolution. Poets like Blake and Wordsworth were inspired by the vision of Druids in sacred groves. William Stukeley was one of the first scholars to attempt to undertake systematic surveys of the megalithic monuments of Avebury and Stonehenge in the mid-18th century, and he attributed both to the Druids, a mistaken belief that persists to the present day. Societies dedicated to the revival of the Druidic religion were founded with imagination building on the scant information that could be gleaned from classical sources. In 1792, a Welsh stonemason named Edward Williams founded the first *Maen Gorsedd*, or 'community of bards', which still forms part of the Welsh National Eisteddfod. Williams, better known by his bardic name, Iolo Morgannwg, also claimed that the Druidic tradition had survived in Wales despite the Roman conquest and the introduction of Christianity. Other eccentric claims were made by James McPherson who published the *Ossianic Poems* in the 1760s, allegedly as a translation of the works of the legendary Ossian, a Gaelic bard who was said to have lived in the early Middle Ages. The poems sold widely throughout Britain and Europe and had a strong influence on the popular image of the Celts at the time before being exposed as forgeries.

Identity and Nationalism

The romantic vision of the Celts has had a particular impact in Scotland. The success of Sir Walter Scott's novel *Rob Roy*, published in 1818, did much to create the popular image of the Gaelic-speaking kilted Highlander. It was also through Scott's efforts that the kilt came to be regarded as the national dress of Scotland, although it was in fact devised almost a century earlier by an English industrialist, Thomas Rawlinson, who wanted his Scottish workers to wear a more practical version of the traditional belted cloak or plaid. The small kilt, or *philabeg*, was quickly adopted by the Lowland aristocracy who were eager to embrace the new Celtic identity of their northern countrymen as a means of emphasizing the differences between all Scots and English. The traditional Scottish tartan is a similar invention of the 19th century. Although tartans are known to have existed in many areas of Europe and Asia for over 3,000 years, and are one of the simplest patterns to weave on a hand-operated loom, the clan tartans in the form we know them today were invented by textile manufacturers in the Lowlands anxious to profit by the new fashion. The bagpipes, another inseparable element of modern Scottish culture, were originally invented in the Middle East and were popular throughout Europe in the Middle Ages. Their survival in Scotland owes much to their adoption by the British Army for its Highland regimental bands and to the enthusiasm of Queen Victoria. The contributions of both the Highlands and the Lowlands to the creation of the cultural symbols of modern Scotland, in which the Celts play an important role, have served to overcome the historical divide and animosity between the two, and in so doing have encouraged the development of a homogeneous Scottish identity.

Bronze statue of the dying Cúchulainn, in Dublin's General Post Office. The rediscovery of the Celts in the 18th century played a major role in the establishment of a modern Celtic national identity in Ireland. (© 2003 Topham Picturepoint / Topfoto)

The rediscovery of the ancient Celts has also defined the development of a modern Irish identity. Unlike Scotland, however, the romantic Celtic revival accentuated rather than lessened the divisions in the country. At the end of the 18th century, the idea of a Celtic national identity had the support of Catholics and Protestants in Ireland. In 1795, a group of Ulster Protestants founded the first society for the preservation of the Irish language. As the 19th century progressed, support grew for the use of Gaelic as a way of asserting 'Irishness' based on a Celtic past as English rule and influence were rejected. Ancient Irish myths and legends, especially the story of Cúchulainn, inspired nationalists such as those of the Fenian Society.

The Protestant minority, mostly descendants of 17th-century settlers from England and the Scottish Lowlands, felt alienated by a growing nationalism that was now increasingly defined by the Catholic majority and increasingly intolerant of their own identity. A consequence of this was Protestant support for Unionism and opposition to Home Rule. The failure of nationalism in Ireland to foster an identity that could encompass both communities was one of the principal factors that led to partition in 1922. The creation of an independent Republic of Ireland and the continuance of the Six Counties of Ulster within the United Kingdom has been only a partial solution to the problem that still exists to this day.

By the mid-19th century, awareness of the Celtic past was also being used by a number of western European countries to enhance their national identities. Celtic leaders who had resisted the domination of Rome began to appear as national heroes in art, sculpture and literature: Vercingetorix in France, Ambiorix in Belgium, and Viriatus in Spain and Portugal. At the same time, a more objective understanding of the Celts was slowly emerging with the development of methodical excavation and recording techniques by amateur archaeologists. The discovery and excavation of the eponymous Celtic sites at Halstatt and La Tène in the 1840s and 1850s are models of their kind. In France in the 1860s, Napoleon III sponsored excavations at Alésia, the scene of heroic resistance by Vercingetorix and the Gauls against Caesar. Apart from the emperor's own personal interest, the project was also intended to encourage national sentiment at a time when France was feeling threatened by the rise of Prussian power in Europe.

The revival and preservation of the Celtic languages have been fundamental to the development of Celtic identity over the last 300 years. Despite this, there has been a continuous decline in the number of Celtic speakers during this period. Forced emigration, famine, official indifference and hostility are all responsible. Active encouragement and financial aid on the part of national governments since the Second World War have done little to remedy the situation. (It is estimated that there are now more Chinese than Irish speakers in Dublin.) The only modern Celtic nation where the native Celtic language is not in decline is Wales. It is clear, therefore, that the modern Celtic identity does not depend on the continued survival

Ambiorix, leader of the Eburones against Caesar, and national hero in Belgium. The statue stands in Tongeren, the oldest town in Belgium, the site of the main settlement of the Tungri. (© Michael Nicholson / CORBIS)

Honoured as a national hero in both Spain and Portugal, this statue of the Lusitanian leader Viriatus stands in the Portuguese town of Viseu. (© 2002 Topham Picturepoint / Topfoto)

of the Celtic languages. Cultural, historical and political factors have become more important. This is well demonstrated by the example of the Spanish province of Gallicia, where a new awareness of its Celtiberian past has led to the recent revival of Celtic identity that owes nothing at all to the question of language. The modern Celtic identity is promoted by communities in response to years, if not centuries, of social, economic and political neglect. The regional policies now being pursued by the European Union have given these communities the opportunity to make their voices heard.

ROMANCE VERSUS REALITY

At the end of the 20th century, the romanticized image of the Celts once more captured popular imagination with the increase in concern for the environment and

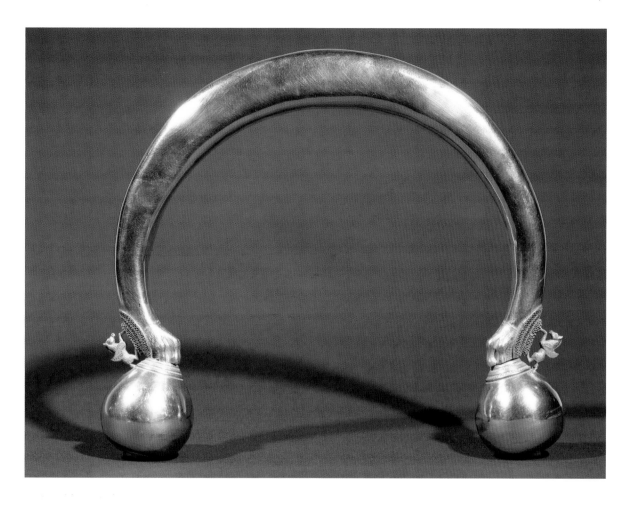

the decline of organized religion. It has been adopted by the more mystical elements among environmentalists and also as one of the mainstays of neo-paganism. In many ways, the Celts have come to represent those things that are lacking in modern society, especially spirituality and a respect for the natural world. Inevitably, perhaps, warfare does not feature prominently in this image. The reality, of course, is that the Celts were a warlike people: warfare was an essential element in the structure and maintenance of ancient Celtic society and was the quickest way to achieve wealth and prestige. The Romans, who made the art of war into a science, paid the Celtic warrior the ultimate accolade by adopting his mail armour, his helmet design and his cavalry saddle. The attitude of the Celts to the natural world was similar to that of all ancient peoples for whom agriculture was the economic basis of their society. It may well have been infused with the supernatural but that did not prevent it from being fully exploited. Religion and spiritual belief pervaded all aspects of their lives,

The solid gold Vix torc, one of the treasures of early Celtic art. (akg-images / Erich Lessing)

but no more so than any other ancient society. Their love of beautiful objects and the status they acquired by the possession and display of such objects is ample proof of their materialism. Celtic women certainly enjoyed greater status, influence and sexual freedom than their sisters in Greece or Rome; marriage was a much more equal partnership. But for all that, Celtic society remained just as male-dominated as its Mediterranean contemporaries.

THE LEGACY OF THE CELTS

The fame and renown gained by the Celtic warrior in life would live on after his death. The heroism and valour of the dead were extolled in song by bards at the feast as an example to the living. Some tales grew in the telling until they became part of Celtic myth and legend. Others remained part of history. In the 6th century AD, the British poet Aneirin wrote a fitting epitaph for all Celtic warriors when he described the men of Manau Gododdin who rode out to meet the Saxons at the battle of Catraeth:

> Three hundred gold-torqued warriors attacked, defending their land ... there was slaughter ... though they were killed, they slew ... and until the end of the world they will be remembered.
> (Y Gododdin)

The Celts have left us a legacy which is only now beginning to be understood and fully appreciated. The intricacy of their art, the beauty of their jewellery and metalwork, the subtlety of their language and the depth of their perception of their world and that of their gods, all confirm their right to be considered as one of the truly great cultures of Europe, comparable to any in the ancient world.

GLOSSARY

Ager gallicus	Region of Italy to the east of the Apennine mountains bordering the Adriatic coast heavily settled by Celtic migrants during the 4th century BC.
Annwn	The Otherworld in Welsh myth and legend.
Bards	Poets who praised or satirized the warrior in song and who recounted the exploits of the heroes of Celtic legend.
Carnyx	Long-necked war horn with a mouth often in the form of an animal.
Celtiberians	The inhabitants of central and northern Spain in the late pre-Roman Iron Age. Apart from their Celtic language, there was little to distinguish them from the Iberian peoples in the south and east of the peninsula.
Celtic migrations	Term given to the large-scale movements of Celtic peoples from west-central Europe to northern Italy and along the Danube basin in the first half of the 4th century BC. Several tribes subsequently settled in Asia Minor. The causes of these migrations remain unclear, though overpopulation is believed to be one of the main factors.
Celts (Greek *Keltoi*, Latin *Celtae*)	Generic name given to the inhabitants of central and western Europe north of the Alps in the late pre-Roman Iron Age (c. 500 BC to c. AD 100). Their origins and how to define them are still a matter of much controversy. They are most commonly defined as those peoples speaking dialects of the Indo-European family of languages now known as Celtic.
Clientage	An agreement of mutual obligation by which a lower-ranking member of Celtic society (the client) would pledge allegiance to an individual of higher rank (the patron) in exchange for security, patronage and employment. A similar system often linked entire clans and tribes.
Devotio	Oath of allegiance sworn by Celtiberian warriors to a leader to die in battle rather than desert or outlive him.
Druids	Privileged class of priests, law givers and guardians of tribal tradition. Known with certainty only in Britain,

where they were said to have originated, and in Gaul. The Galatoi had tribal judges who probably fulfilled a similar role.

Drunemeton	Translates as 'oak sanctuary'. A grove of oak trees ('drus' – oak) held to be particularly sacred to the Celts.
Equites	The 'knightly class' of the Roman Republic.
Excarnation	The process whereby a corpse is exposed to the elements or temporarily buried until the flesh has rotted from the bones, which are then reburied and/or used in further ritual.
Falcata	Sabre with heavy curved blade used by Iberian and Celtiberian warriors.
Gaesatae	'Spear-bearers' hence 'warriors' because in Celtic society a man who bore a spear belonged to that class whose role was to fight. Compare 'ash-bearers' in early Anglo-Saxon society (spears were often made of ash wood). A large group of Celtic mercenary warriors who crossed the Alps to join the Celtic tribes of northern Italy in their struggle against Rome in the late 3rd century BC. Characterized by their practice of fighting naked.
Gaesum	A large Celtic spear.
Galatoi (Galatians)	Greek name given to the Celtic tribes who settled in Asia Minor after the defeat of the Celts in Greece in the first half of the 3rd century BC.
Galli (Gauls)	Roman name given to the Celtic peoples in northern Italy and France.
Geissi	Taboos or sacred rules of conduct imposed on or voluntarily accepted by the Celtic warrior.
Halstatt	Archaeological site in Austria discovered in the early 19th century. The finds from the site were identified as belonging to the early pre-Roman Iron Age (c. 8th to 5th centuries BC) to which it gave its name. The Halstatt period is now considered to extend back into the late Bronze Age (from c. 1200 BC), but it is mainly characterized by early Iron Age princedoms – centres of power in eastern France and southern Germany. With the introduction

	of ironworking technology from the 8th century BC onwards, many of the elements of Celtic culture began to appear.
La Tène	Archaeological site in Switzerland discovered in the mid-19th century. Believed to have been a religious sanctuary, the rich finds at La Tène were identified as similar to others from northern France and the Rhineland, areas that rose to prominence following the collapse of the Halstatt Princedoms. The later pre-Roman Iron Age is now referred to as the La Tène period and the name is widely associated with the material culture of the Celts.
Men of Art	Irish term given to the class in Celtic society that included artisans, metalworkers, bards and Druids.
Oppidum (pl. oppida)	A large, often fortified urban centre.
Potlach	Ostentatious distribution or redistribution of prestige items such as gold or wine among a warrior's retinue or to others in general, often given in the context of the feast to enhance the giver's status.
Stelae	Upright stone slabs or pillars usually with inscriptions and sculptures marking ritual or burial sites.
Symposion	The ritual wine-drinking ceremony of the Greeks. Many of its characteristics were adopted by the Celts and incorporated into their own feasting.
Testudo	Roman infantry formation in which troops protect themselves from enemy missiles by presenting their shields to their front, sides and above their heads.
Tir na n'Og	The Otherworld in Irish myth and legend.
Torc	Neck ring, usually made of finely worked gold or other precious metals. Worn as a symbol of rank by high-status warriors and probably of ritual significance.
Trimarcisia	Translates as 'group of three horsemen' and has its origins in the word *macha* ('horse'). Term used to describe a Celtic manner of fighting on horseback whereby the mounted warrior is supported by two retainers who provide him with a fresh horse, protect him if wounded and replace him in battle as required.
Woad	A plant from which a blue dye was extracted that was used by Britons to paint or tattoo their bodies.

BIBLIOGRAPHY

PRIMARY SOURCES

The quotations from classical authors are translations from the *Loeb Classical Library* series unless otherwise indicated.

Ammianus Marcellinus, *The Late Roman Empire* (tr. W. Hamilton, Penguin Classics, 1986)

Aneirin, *Y Gododdin*, (tr. K. H. Jackson, Edinburgh University Press, 1969)

Appian, *Roman History* (tr. H. White, 1912)

Athenaeus, *Deipnosophistae* (tr. C. Gulick, 1928)

Avienus, *Ora Maritima* (tr. J. Murphy, Ares, 1977)

Caesar, *The Conquest of Gaul* (tr. S. Handford, Penguin Classics, 1951)

Cassius Dio, *Roman History* (tr. E. Cary, 1914)

Diodorus Siculus, *Historical Library* (tr. C. Oldfather, 1933)

Herodotus, *Histories* (tr. A. Godley, 1924)

Livy, *History of Rome* (tr. B. Foster, 1924)

Lucan, *The Civil War* (tr. J. Duff, 1928)

Pausanias, *Description of Greece* (tr. W. Jones and H. Ormerod, 1926)

Plutarch, *Lives* (tr. B. Perrin, 1914)

Polybius, *The Histories* (tr. W. Paton, 1922)

Strabo, *Geography* (tr. H. Jones, 1917)

Tacitus, *Agricola* (tr. H. Mattingly, Penguin Classics, 1948) and *Annals* (tr. J. Jackson, 1931)

Xenophon, *Hellenica* (tr. C. Brownson, 1918)

SECONDARY SOURCES

Allen, Stephen, *Celtic Warrior*, Osprey (2001)

Collins, John, *The European Iron Age*, Batsford (1992)

Cunliffe, Barry, *Greeks, Romans and Barbarians*, Batsford (1988)

Cunliffe, Barry, *Iron Age Britain*, Batsford (1993)

Cunliffe, Barry (ed.), *The Oxford Illustrated Prehistory of Europe*, Oxford University Press (1994)

Cunliffe, Barry, *The Ancient Celts*, Oxford University Press (1997)

Cunliffe, Barry, *Facing the Ocean*, Oxford University Press (2001)

Cunliffe, Barry, *The Celts, A Very Short Introduction*, Oxford University Press (2003)

Gantz, J. (tr.), *Mabinogion*, Penguin Classics (1976)

Gantz, J. (tr.), *Early Irish Myths and Sagas*, Penguin Classics (1981)

Green, Miranda, *Celtic Myths*, British Museum Press (1993)

Green, Miranda (ed.), *The Celtic World*, Routledge (1995)

Green, Miranda, *Exploring the World of the Druids*, Thames and Hudson (1997)

Haywood, John, *The Historical Atlas of the Celtic World*,
    Thames and Hudson (2001)

Haywood, John, *The Celts – Bronze Age to New Age*, Longman (2004)

Jackson, K. H. (tr.), *A Celtic Miscellany*, Penguin Classics (1973)

James, Simon, *Exploring the World of the Celts*, Thames and Hudson (1993)

James, Simon, *The Atlantic Celts*, British Museum Press (1999)

Jones, Martin, *The Molecule Hunt*, Allen Lane, The Penguin Press (2001)

Kinsela, T. (tr.), *Táin Bó Cuailnge*, Oxford University Press (1970)

Kristiansen, Kristian, *Europe Before History*, Cambridge University Press (1998)

Kruta, Venseslas, *Les Celtes*, Presses Universitaires de France (2002)

Kruta, Venseslas, *Celts, History and Civilisation*, Hachette (2004)

Powell, T. G. E., *The Celts*, Thames and Hudson (1980)

Ritchie, W. F. and J. N. G., *Celtic Warriors*, Shire (1985)

Solway, Peter, *Roman Britain*, Oxford University Press (1981)

Stead, I. M., *Celtic Art*, British Museum Press (1993)

Tolkien, J. R. R., *Angles and Britons: O'Donnell Lectures*,
    University of Cardiff Press (1963)

Treviño Martinez, Rafael, *Rome's Enemies (4): Spanish Armies*, Osprey (1986)

Wells, Peter, *Beyond Celts, Germans and Scythians*, Duckworth (2001)

Wilcox, Peter, *Rome's Enemies (2): Gallic and British Celts*, Osprey (1985)

INDEX

References to illustrations are shown in **bold**.